ПУШКИН И ЕГО ДРУЗЬЯ

An Exhibition of
the Kilgour Collection

Selection and Commentaries by John E. Malmstad

with Introductory Prefaces by William Mills Todd III

The Houghton Library
Cambridge · 1987

PUSHKIN
AND HIS FRIENDS
The Making of a Literature and a Myth

Sources

All entries and illustrations are from books given by, or bought with funds provided by, Mr. Kilgour, except the following:

C. R. Carne 11
Philip Hofer Cover, frontispiece, 10b, 13, 77b–c
Baron R. R. Osten Sacken 73
Peabody fund 71
Sheldon fund 34
Charles Sumner 43

Uncaptioned illustrations (excluding those identified in text)
Cover: from Vingt-quatre nouvelles vues de Saint-Petersbourg (SPb., 1822)
Frontispiece: "L'eglise du palais a Tzarskoé-selo," from Joseph Meyer (b. 1808), *Vues pittoresques des palais et jardins imperiaux aux environs de St. Petersbourg* (SPb. & Paris, [ca. 1850?])
Title page: from no. 28 (frontispiece)
p. 16, 49: from no. 5 (tailpieces)
p. 25: from no. 57, v. 1 (tailpiece)
p. 32: ex libris Bayard L. Kilgour, Jr.
p. 52: from no. 44 (title vignette)
p. 75: fron no. 69 (title vignette)
p. 87: from no. 54 (tailpiece)
p. 95: no. 24 (title page)

Design by Richard C. Bartlett, Cotuit, Mass.; photography by Victor Santamaria, Daniel Sullivan, and Rick Stafford; type by Crane Typesetting Service, Inc., Barnstable, Mass.; printing by the Office of the University Publisher, Harvard University.

THE EXHIBITION AND CATALOGUE
ARE DEDICATED TO BAYARD L. KILGOUR, JR. '27
(1904–1984)
FOUNDER AND SUPPORTER
OF THE HARVARD COLLECTION OF
RUSSIAN BELLES LETTRES

NOTE

That this assemblage of books and manuscripts by one of the world's great poets could exist outside his homeland will puzzle all Russians; and, that virtually everything in this exhibition was given to his alma mater by a single American amateur will confound all specialist scholars — unless they know the name of Kilgour.

Before he entered Harvard with the class of 1927 Bayard Livingston Kilgour, Jr., of Cincinnati had been impressed by his adventuresome, world-travelling mother, who told him to watch Russia: in his time its star would rise. At Harvard his faculty friends A. C. Coolidge and R. P. Blake encouraged his interest. By graduation he had already visited the country of his dreams in quest of books.

Then, in 1952, he gave to Harvard the collection that dazzled the world when the catalogue was published in 1959, certainly a standard that may never be equalled or surpassed. Three generations of Harvard librarians have been inspired by Bayard Kilgour's generous determination to build and improve the collection, doing all they could to find books and manuscripts worthy of his name.

Kate Gray Kilgour, his loving wife and devoted widow, has continued his work by offering funds for acquisitions and for this catalogue, the exhibition opening and receptions.

Harvard friends — faculty, librarians and students — salute Bayard and Kate Kilgour; striving through teaching, studies and scholarship, they will fulfill the hopes that the Kilgours have vouchsafed by placing the great collection here.

ROGER E. STODDARD
Curator of Rare Books

INTRODUCTION

This year marks the one hundred and fiftieth anniversary of the death from traumatic peritonitis of Aleksandr Sergeevich Pushkin, at 2:45 p.m. on 29 January 1837, forty-five hours after he received a wound to the lower abdomen during a duel fought outside St. Petersburg, at the ominously named Chernaia Rechka (Black Brook). By the 1830's, after a decade of unprecedented critical and popular acclaim, Pushkin seemed destined to play the role of a doormat for the coming generation to step on. The reading public and critics from every camp greeted his new works with incomprehension or outright hostility, while younger writers looked elsewhere for inspiration. His tragically premature death at the hands of Baron Georges d'Anthès, a minor French émigré nobleman, acting, it was widely (and erroneously) believed, at the instigation or at least with the connivance of the Government and Court society, largely stilled the detractors and brought him the absolute respect and "centrality" he had struggled for so vainly in life. The Government, which had so feared hostile public demonstrations that it insisted on a secret funeral service and interment far from the capital, could try to minimize the outpouring of public grief and could exile the young Lermontov for his accusatory "Death of a Poet." It could do nothing to stop the beginning of a myth, whose Ptolemaic outlines first appeared in an unsigned note in the Sunday issue (No. 25–26) of the Petersburg newspaper *The Russian Invalid* only two days after the death: "The Sun of our Poetry has set! *Pushkin* has died, died in the prime of life, in the middle of his great career! . . . We lack the strength to speak of it any more, but then there is no need to. Every Russian heart knows the full cost of this irrevocable loss, and every Russian heart will be rent by it. *Pushkin*! Our poet! Our joy, our national glory! . . . Can it really be that *Pushkin* is no longer among us? . . . It is impossible to get used to this idea!"

That Sun has never since been eclipsed, despite a few attempts over the years to cloud it, and no one has ever succeeded in challenging Pushkin's exclusive hold on the romantic title of "national poet"—"our all, our everything," as the sober and always hard-headed Vladislav Khodasevich put it. If a German speaks of Goethe or an Englishman of Shakespeare, a Russian will salute Pushkin, and will insist on his national and universal qualities, as did Igor Stravinsky, for example, in his 1936 *Autobiography*: "By his nature, his mentality, and his ideology Pushkin was the most perfect representative of that wonderful line which began with Peter the Great and which, by a fortunate alloy, has united the most characteristically Russian elements with the spiritual riches of the West."

Russians of every cultural and political stripe have vied for the sole right to claim Pushkin's legacy and have disagreed fiercely over its meaning, but they have united to celebrate anniversaries of his birth and death ever since the late nineteenth century with "Pushkin Days" or "Days of Russian Culture", so closely is the writer equated with national cultural identity. Major dates obviously call for special efforts. Preparations for the hundredth anniversary of his death began well before 1937, and it was marked worldwide with concerts, theater performances, special editions (in every major language), exhibitions, newly commissioned operas based on his works, and solemn meetings, as well as with movies, commemorative medals and postage stamps. Some of the books on display here — those from the Diaghilev-Lifar collection — were shown at the Exposition Pouchkine assembled by Serge Lifar in the Salle Pleyel in Paris; the H. W. L. Dana Collection in the Harvard Theatre Collection contains numerous materials on celebrations of the event all over America, 31 January – 20 February 1937, including a special concert of the Boston Symphony conducted by Koussevitzky and a program of speeches at Harvard.

1987 has witnessed festivities on almost as grand a scale in the Soviet Union. Western tributes have largely been confined to scholarly conferences. There seemed no better way for Harvard to mark the occasion than with an exhibition of books. Pushkin died in his study literally surrounded by favorite volumes from his library, and among his last words was a touching farewell to them. Many can be seen here because of the extraordinary collecting passion and generosity of Bayard L. Kilgour, Jr., '27, who built for Harvard a collection of Russian literature unrivalled in the West. Almost every volume on display has been drawn from his gifts to the Houghton Library. Selecting only some eighty titles from those riches proved no easy task. The result, ranging from the *Lay of the Host of Igor* (the "birthdate" of Russian literature for Pushkin) and significant predecessors and contemporaries to Pushkin's own writings (the Kilgour collection contains every first edition) and landmarks of their scholarly publication and his canonization, presents, I think, a picture of the writer and the literary, material, and institutional circumstances in which he labored. The commentary, too, focuses on Pushkin himself, whom, after all, we honor, by citations from his critical writings, journals, autobiographical manuscripts, and, above all, the letters where his difficult and problematical character most vividly revealed itself. It would be hard to imagine Pushkin's biography without the versions of himself he disseminated through the mail with such unflagging verve. The sense of literature as a way of life has as much gone out of fashion as has the habit of writing letters. For Pushkin, letters were simply another mode of literary expression, and they belonged to the writer's vocation to which he had apprenticed himself every bit as much as verse, fiction, or essays. His family is also represented in a sense by Natalia Goncharova's brilliant designs (from the Harvard Theatre Collection), for the *Coq d'Or*, Fokine's ballet, to Rimsky-Korsakov's operatic setting of "The Tale of the Golden Cockerel," revived at Covent Garden in 1937 by Colonel de Basil. Pushkin's wife, another Natalia Goncharova, was a cousin of the artist's great-grandfather.

Several people besides Bayard L. Kilgour, Jr. and his family (who made the catalogue possible) need to be thanked. William Mills Todd III, Professor of Slavic and Comparative Literature at Stanford, provided, at very short notice, critical and historical introductions for nine of the exhibition's ten sections (signed "WMT"). Roger E. Stoddard gave his enthusiastic support to my initial proposal and helped ensure its realization. Hugh Amory meticulously edited the catalogue entries and brought his practised eye to bear on the selection of illustrative material. The patient assistance and professional courtesy of the staff of the Houghton Reading Room during the long selection process deserve special acknowledgement. They had to bring hundreds of books from the repositories and they never grumbled when most were looked at only for a few minutes before being sent back for reshelving accompanied by requests for yet more volumes.

Some final technical points remain. Russian names, places, titles, and texts appear in the Roman alphabet according to the Library of Congress system of transliteration, with these exceptions: 1) surnames appear with the ending *-sky* (Zhukovsky); 2) names of familiar authors, historical figures, and literary characters appear in their usual spelling (Gogol, Alexander I, *Eugene Onegin*); 3) names of foreign origin in most cases appear according to the spelling of the original ethnic group (Benckendorff). All titles are rendered in the new orthography.

John E. Malmstad
Professor of Slavic Languages
and Literatures,
Harvard University

References

Diaghilev-Lifar Library Sotheby Parke Bernet, Monaco (Serge Lifar) 28 novembre 1975; cited by lot number.

Kilgour Harvard College Library. *The Kilgour Collection of Russian Literature, 1750-1920*. Cambridge, 1959.

Nabokov ASP, *Eugene Onegin*, tr. Vladimir Nabokov, v. 2–3 (commentary). New York, 1964

СЛОВО

О ПЪЛКУ ИГОРЕВѢ (а)
ИГОРЯ СЫНА
СВЯТЪСЛАВЛЯ
ВНУКА ОЛЬГОВА.

Не лѣполи ны бяшетъ, братіе, начяти старыми словесы трудныхъ повѣстій о пълку Игоревѣ, Игоря Святъславлича! начати же ся тъй пѣсни по

ПѢСНЬ

О ПОХОДѢ ИГОРЯ
СЫНА СВЯТОСЛАВОВА,
ВНУКА ОЛЬГОВА.

Пріятно намъ, братцы, начать древнимъ слогомъ прискорбную повѣсть о походѣ Игоря, сына Святославова! начать же сію пѣснь по бытіямъ того времени, а не по

(а) *Игорь Святославичъ* родился 15 Апрѣля 1151 года; во Святомъ Крещеніи нареченъ *Георгій*; женился въ 1184 году на Княжнѣ *Евфросиніи*, дочери Князя Ярослава Володимировича *Галичьскаго*. — Въ 1185 году имѣлъ сраженіе съ Половцами, а въ 1201 году скончался, оставивъ послѣ себя пять сыновей.

No.

·I·

MODES OF PUBLICATION

The Age of Pushkin was also the age in which Russian literature began to come to maturity as a secular institution. During the first decades of the nineteenth century Pushkin and his most talented, foresighted contemporaries managed not only to write memorable lyrics, plays, stories, histories, and critical essays, but also to pull together the disparate, isolated attempts of their eighteenth-century predecessors to found a secular literature, create a language for it, establish publishing enterprises, synthesize Western and native traditions, and meet the interests of the small but active readership that had been created by the Westward-oriented reforms of the Petrine era, a readership even smaller than the five percent of the population that is estimated to have enjoyed some degree of literacy.

A representative list of titles shows the period's obsession with literature as an actual or potential institution: Karamzin, "Why There are Few Authorial Talents in Russia" (1802) and "On the Book Trade and On the Love for Reading in Russia" (1802); Zhukovsky, "The Writer in Society" (1809); Pushkin, "A Conversation between a Bookseller and a Poet" (1824); Gogol, "On the Development of Periodical Literature in 1834 and 1835" (1836); Lermontov, "Journalist, Reader, and Writer" (1840). Essays and works of literature by these and other writers addressed every conceivable aspect of literature as an institution: the status of the writer; the reader's role in the literary process; the proper subjects and language for literature; literature as a mode of association; literature and social concerns; literature and the marketplace; censorship.

The literary institutions of early nineteenth-century Russia—the sponsorship of the Autocrat and his government, the salons and familiar groups of the enlightened Westernized gentry, the chapbook trade (*lubok*), and incipient professionalism (journals, almanacs, purchases by booksellers)—offered a gentleman-writer such as Pushkin no easy solution to the problem of realizing exceptional authorial talent and playing an enlightening role in society while preserving noble independence from bureaucratic and commercial subservience. A respected older contemporary, Nikolai Karamzin, had approached this goal by combining the possibilities that these institutions offered: as official historiographer, he was protected from the censorship by the Tsar; as a landowner and writer whose works found favor with the public, he was freed financially from the necessity of state service; as a leading practitioner of the salon style, indeed as one of its creators, he was welcomed in polite society. And Pushkin took cognizance of Karamzin's place amid these institutions in a penetrating article, "Fragments of Letters, Thoughts, and Comments" (1827). Yet Pushkin's own attempts to chart a similar course ended in a disastrous parody of the Karamzinian synthesis. The 3,000 rubles that he received for his narrative poem "The Fountain of Bakhchisarai" (1824) had been the largest honorarium ever paid to a Russian poet, and this success paralleled the success of Karamzin's *History of the Russian State*. But as such financial successes of the 1820's gave way to nearly hopeless attempts to establish periodicals of high quality (*The Literary Gazette*, *The Contemporary*), to bitter literary quarrels with rival journalists, to humiliation at court instead of the Autocrat's respectful attention, and to the vicious social intrigues that led to his death in a duel, Pushkin's early optimism yielded to sober reflections on the state of Russian culture.

The materials in the first floor case and in the first wall case illustrate the institutional possibilities of Russian literature in Pushkin's youth: products of the patronage system, which supported educational projects and literary works of high prestige (Lomonosov's *Rhetoric*, Karamzin's *History*, Gnedich's translation of the *Iliad*); the virtually anonymous, poorly paid, but widely accessible fruits of the chapbook trade (Orlov's *The Devil's Nights*); and the privately printed or manuscript texts of the salons and student circles (Zhukovsky's *Für Wenige* and Volkonskaia's album). Karamzin's collection, *Aglaia*, is an early attempt at remunerated literary activity by a representative of salon culture. The remaining woodcuts show how the works of this polite culture could be absorbed and disseminated by the system of mass literature; the edition of Baratynsky's *The Concubine* shows how one serious author tried to avoid this fate. The edition of *The Lay of the Host of Igor* and Karamzin's article on it illustrate one movement in the contemporary search for an appropriable literary past; Gnedich's translation represents another aspect of this search, the period's attempts to assimilate the achievements of other times and cultures.

W M T

1

The Lay of the host of Igor.

Iroicheskaia pesn' o pokhode na Polovtsov udel'nogo kniazia novagoroda-severskogo Igoria Sviatoslavicha.
Moscow, 1800.

Kilgour 452

In a survey "*Lettre au Spectateur sur la littérature russe*," written at the request of the editor of *Le Spectateur du Nord* and published in its October, 1797 issue, Nikolai Karamzin (signing himself "N. N.") announced to the West a discovery demonstrating that Russian letters could boast of a history no less ancient and distinguished than those of Europe:

> But what will perhaps come as more of a surprise, Monsieur, is that two years ago a fragment of a poem called *The Song of the Warriors of Igor* was unearthed in our archives, and that this song, which was done in the twelfth century by an unknown author, may perhaps be compared to the finest fragments of Ossian. An energetic style, sentiments of sublime heroism, striking images drawn from horrifying aspects of nature [*les horreurs de la nature*], distinguish this fragment, where the poet, tracing a picture of bloody battle, cries; "Ah! I feel my brush fail and languish; I do not have the talent of the great Bayan, that nightingale of the past!" Thus we find that there were great poets in Russia before him, whose works are swallowed up by the centuries! Our annals do not mention this Bayan; we

> know nothing, neither when he lived, nor what he sang. But this hommage, bestowed on his genius by such a poet, makes us deeply regret the loss of his works.

Questions about the authenticity of the work, discovered in a collection of ancient manuscripts acquired in 1795 by the statesman and amateur archeologist Count Aleksei Ivanovich Musin-Pushkin (1744–1817; the Counts Musin-Pushkin were distantly related to Pushkin's family), immediately arose both in Russia and abroad. Pushkin took a lively interest in the controversy, which continues to this day, and he never doubted the *Lay*'s genuineness. In the beginning of 1836 he began an article, perhaps intended for an annotated edition of the *Lay* he hoped to publish, that remained unfinished at the time of his death:

> *The Song of the Host of Igor* was found in the library of Count A. I. Musin-Pushkin and was published in 1800. The manuscript was burned in 1812. Experts who have seen it say that its script was semi-cursive, of the fifteenth century. Its first publishers appended a translation, which was on the whole satisfactory, although several places remained obscure or altogether unintelligible. Many people subsequently tried to elucidate them. But, although in researches of this kind the last becomes the first (since the mistakes and discoveries of their predecessors open up and clear the way for those that follow), the first translation, in which truly learned men [A. F. Malinovsky and N. N. Bantysh-Kamensky] took part, still remains the best . . . .
>
> A few writers doubted the genuineness of this ancient monument of our poetry and raised heated protests. A happy forgery can deceive the ignorant, but it cannot escape the scrutiny of a real expert. Walpole was not deceived when Chatterton sent him the poems of the old monk Rowley; Johnson immediately exposed Macpherson; but neither Karamzin, nor Ermolaev, nor A. Kh. Vostokov, nor Khodakovsky ever doubted the genuineness of *The Song of the Host of Igor*. The great critic Schlözer, before he had seen *The Song of the Host of Igor*, had doubts about its authenticity, but having read it, he emphatically declared that he regarded it as a genuinely ancient work and he did not even consider it necessary to adduce any proof of this, so obvious did the truth seem to him!
>
> There is no other proof except the words of the poet himself. For the authenticity of the song itself is proved by its spirit of antiquity, which cannot be forged. Which of our eighteenth-century writers had enough talent for that? Karamzin? But Karamzin is not a poet. Derzhavin? But Derzhavin did not even know the Russian language, let alone that of *The Song of the Host of Igor*. The others all combined had not as much poetry in them as is found in Iaroslavna's lament, and in the description of the battle and flight. To whom would it have occurred to take as the subject for a song an obscure expedition by an unknown prince! Who could have obscured with such skill certain places in his song by using words since discovered in ancient chronicles or traced in other Slavic dialects, where they are still preserved in all the freshness of common usage? That would assume a knowledge of all Slavic dialects. Let us suppose someone were to possess all of them, would such a jumble be natural? Homer, if he even existed, was distorted by rhapsodists.
>
> Lomonosov did not live in the twelfth century. Lomonosov's odes are written in Russian, with an admixture of certain expressions taken from the Bible, which lay open before him. But you will not find in Lomonosov either Polish, or Serbian, or Illyrian, or Bulgarian, or Bohemian, or Moldavian, etc. or any other Slavic dialect.

Pushkin's comments on random passages of *The Lay* and on various translations of it follow in the article.

The *editio princeps*, which occupies forty-six pages with a parallel version in modern Russian, appeared on 5 December 1800 in a volume whose full title reads (in translation), "The Heroic Song of the Campaign Against the Polovtsy of the Territorial Prince of Novgorod-Seversk, Igor Sviatoslavich, Written in the Ancient Russian Language at the Close of the Twelfth Century, with a Transposition into the Idiom Now in Use." It and an apograph made from the manuscript for Catherine II are now our only authority for the text. On display is the extremely rare first issue with no cancelled leaves, first described in *Harvard Library Bulletin*, VI, 1952. The volume is open to a folding genealogical table of the princes mentioned in the text, which was included in this and the second issue (also in the Kilgour collection). Also on display is the Óctober 1797 issue of *Le Spectateur du Nord* open to the beginning of Karamzin's "Letter."

2

Mikhail Vasil'evich Lomonosov (1711–65),
A brief guide to rhetoric.

Kratkoe rukovodstvo k krasnorechiiu.
St. Petersburg, 1748.

Kilgour 654

In his 1825 article "On Monsieur Lémontey's Introduction to the Translation of I. A. Krylov's *Fables*" (*Moscow Telegraph*, Pt. V, No. 17), Pushkin took exception to Lémontey's treatment of "the outstanding comrade-in-arms of the great Peter." Lémontey had stressed Lomonosov's poetic achievement; Pushkin placed the emphasis elsewhere:

> Combining uncommon will-power with uncommon powers of understanding, Lomonosov embraced all branches of enlightenment. The thirst for learning was the strongest passion of this spirit charged with passions. Historian, rhetorician, mechanic, chemist, mineralogist, artist and poet, he experienced and penetrated everything: he was the first to delve deeply into our country's history, to establish the rules of its public language, to draw up laws and give models of classical rhetoric, . . . and finally, to reveal to us the true sources of our poetic language. Poetry may be the sole passion of a few born poets. It embraces and absorbs all their observations, all their efforts, and all the impressions of their lives; but when we begin to study Lomonosov's life we will find that the exact sciences were always his main and favorite pursuit, while the writing of poetry, though at times a diversion, was more often for him an official exercise. We would search in vain for ardent outbursts of feeling and imagination in our first lyric poet. His style, even, figurative and picturesque, takes its chief merit from his profound knowledge of written Slavic and from his happy mingling of the colloquial with it. That is why his renderings of the Psalms and his other vigorous and close imitations of the exalted poetry of the Scriptures are his finest works. They will remain eternal memorials of Russian literature; for a long time to come we will have to learn our poetic language from them; but it is strange to complain that people of society do not read Lomonosov, and to expect that a man who died seventy years ago should continue to be the public's favorite to this day. As if the great Lomonosov's fame needed the trivial honors of the fashionable writer!

In the same year, in a letter to Aleksandr Bestuzhev (end of May/beginning of June), Pushkin remarked succinctly: "I respect him as a great man, but, of course, not as a great poet. He understood the true source of the Russian language and its beauty: that is his main contribution." Pushkin's antipathy for Lomonosov's verse remained as constant as his respect for his universal genius, as one of his last statements makes clear: "Lomonosov was a great man. Between Peter I and Catherine II he stands alone as an original champion of enlightenment. He founded our first university. Or, to put it better, he was himself our first university. But in this university the Professor of Poetry and Rhetoric was no more than a meticulous official, not a poet inspired from above or an orator who can powerfully fascinate" ("A Journey from Moscow to Petersburg," 1833–34; published posthumously).

In Pushkin's youth the *Brief Guide*, published by the Imperial Academy of Sciences, a major sponsor of scholarly works, was still a common school text. This very rare copy is open to one of the fragments (I,1–7; II,1–4) of the initial text of the "Khotin Ode" ("Ode to the Sovereign of Blessed Memory Anna Ioannovna on the Victory over the Turks and Tartars and on the Taking of Khotin," 1739) which Lomonosov included in the *Guide*. This ode is considered the "birthdate" of Russian poetry and was hailed as such by Vladislav Khodasevich (1886-1939), one of the finest Russian twentieth-century poets (and an important Pushkinist), in an unfinished salute to the iambic tetrameter:

> The years have eroded from memory
> Who perished at Khotin, and why,
> But the first sound of the Khotin ode
> Became our life's first cry.
>
> (1938)

3

Nikolai Mikhailovich Karamzin (1766–1826), *editor*,

***Aglaia*, Books I and II. Moscow, 1794-95.**

Diaghilev-Lifar library 6

When Nikolai Karamzin, a major reformer and reshaper of the Russian literary language as well as of the Russian national consciousness, published the two books of this first Russian literary miscellany in 1794 and 1795 (the second edition of 1796 is also in the Kilgour collection), he began a fashion which lasted, with some interruptions and modifications, well into the twentieth century. In 1796 he himself gave this sort of enterprise its more lasting form with his *Almanakh Aonid* (*Almanac of the Aonids*), an imitation of the famous French *Almanach des muses*. The almanacs were elegant pocket-sized volumes offering a broad selection of short works in verse and prose to the people of fashion who could afford them and who would discuss their contents at the salons and soirées of the time. They appeared shortly before the New Year and rarely for more than a year or two in succession. By the late 1820's these collections had come to dominate Russian publishing. In an 1827 draft of a review of *The Northern Lyre for 1827*, Pushkin wrote: "Almanacs have become the representatives of our literature. In time its movement and successes will be judged with reference to them." If by the 1830's the form had fallen in the esteem of serious writers, who now turned to the founding of literary reviews, it never entirely lost its popularity or outlived its usefulness. The Russian Symbolists seriously revived the tradition (and even the name of Del'vig's *Northern Flowers*) at the end of the century in their successful attempt to find an audience for the "new literature." Even the tradition-bashing Futurists cultivated the form with outrageous gusto. The "croaked moon" might well have been their verdict on the marked Sentimentalist bias of Karamzin's 1794–95 progenitor of the literary collection.

Book I of *Aglaia*, with an epigraph from Charles Bonnet, the Genevan philosopher whose *La Contemplation de la nature* Karamzin translated, and Book II, with an epigraph from Montaigne, may be considered Karamzin's one-man show and publication, although, typically, his name appears after only one piece ("From the Author"). He included in Book I a poem (signed "I. D.") by his principal correspondent, the future Minister of Justice, Ivan Dmitriev (1760–1837) and another (signed "M. ———v") by Mikhail Kheraskov (1733–1807), author of the celebrated 1779 epic *The Rossiada*. Otherwise, *Aglaia* presented Karamzin in nearly all his guises: the sentimental poet, storyteller ("The Island of Bornholm"), traveller (excerpts from *The Letters of A Russian Traveller*), enlightener (the essay "What is Necessary for an Author?"), and philosopher. In both books Karamzin pointedly remarked: "There are only Russian works; there are no translations."

4

N. M. Karamzin,
History of the Russian state.

Istoriia gosudarstva rossiiskogo.
v. 1–8.
St. Petersburg, 1818.

Kilgour 495

In 1803 Karamzin was awarded an annual pension of 2,000 rubles as official historiographer, and he retired from other literary work. The publication in the beginning of 1818 of the first eight volumes of his "romantic-national" *History* met with ecstatic critical praise accompanied by unprecedented popular success. Zhukovsky twice heard Karamzin read sections of the work at meetings of the Arzamas Society in February 1816, and he recognized Karamzin's ennobling of a specifically Russian past. He wrote to Ivan Dmitriev: "What perfection! What an epoch for a Russian when this *History* appears! What a treasure for language and poetry. . . . One may call this *History* the *resurrector of the past ages of our people's existence*."

In an autobiographical fragment on Karamzin (published only posthumously, but used by Pushkin for the "Fragments of Letters, Thoughts and Comments," *Northern Flowers for 1828*), Pushkin recalled the enthusiasm of his first encounter with Karamzin's volumes and their "motley jumble" of notes: "I greedily and attentively read them in bed. The book's appearance caused much commotion and made a powerful impression (as well it should have). Three thousand copies [nearly three times a usual print run] sold out in a month (something Karamzin himself in no way expected). . . . Everyone, even ladies of society, rushed to read the hitherto unknown history of their fatherland. It was a new discovery for them. Ancient Russia, it seemed, was discovered by Karamzin as America by Columbus. For a time no one talked of anything else."

Not long after, Pushkin, displeased with the conservative and pro-autocratic ideology of the work, penned an epigram which wounded Karamzin, but not seriously enough to cause a rupture in his relations with the impetuous young poet:

> In his *History*, elegance and simplicity
> Prove to us, with utter impartiality,
> The necessity of despotism
> And the charm of the knout.

In the late 1820's, as detractors from the Right and Left turned on Karamzin, Pushkin invariably rose to his defense. In the same autobiographical fragment, he went on: "None among us was in a position to analyze and appraise Karamzin's huge creation, but then no one said thank you to this man who had closeted himself in his study during the period of his most flattering successes and had devoted twelve whole years of his life to silent and tireless labors. The notes bear witness to Karamzin's broad learning, acquired by him at that age when for ordinary people the circle of education and knowledge has long closed and occupational cares replace striving for enlightenment. . . . Many forgot that Karamzin published his *History* in Russia, and that the Tsar, having freed him from the censorship, imposed upon Karamzin by this sign of trust an obligation to be as modest and moderate as possible. He told his story with all the truth of the historian, he everywhere referred to his sources—what more can one demand of him? I repeat, the *History of the Russian State* is not only the work of a great writer, but the feat of an *honnête homme*."

Pushkin, like writers for generations after, used the *History* as a source for numerous works. Its twelfth volume, the last Karamzin managed to complete, appeared posthumously in 1829, and the *History* served as an important school text throughout the rest of the century. Academician D. S. Likhachev has recently called for its republication as a "monument" of Russian cultural history, and the popular journal *Ogonek* has announced plans to issue the complete work in a series of special supplements. There has never been a Soviet edition of the entire *History*, but it now seems to be contributing to the recent reemergence of Russian national feeling and self-examination.

The first eight volumes of the Kilgour set are bound in red morocco and bear the book stamps of the Imperial Library of Tsarskoe Selo. A note in the first volume (on display here) states that Karamzin presented this set to Alexander I, to whom the *History* is dedicated and at whose expense the first eight volumes were printed. Although there is no personal inscription, this was probably the Tsar's personal set. Vols. 10–11 are exhibited in case VI (no. 39).

5

Vasilii Andreevich Zhukovsky (1783–1852),
For the few.

***Für Wenige = Dlia nemnogikh*. 6 nos. Moscow, 1818.**

Kilgour 1293

When Zhukovsky met the young Pushkin, still a student at the Lycée de l'Empereur Alexandre I, at Tsarskoe Selo (now Pushkin) in September 1815, he wrote to Viazemsky: "I have made another agreeable acquaintance! With our young wonder-worker Pushkin. I visited him for a minute at Tsarskoe Selo. A charming, lively creature. . . . This is the hope of our literature. . . . We must all unite to help see that this future giant, who is going to outstrip us all, develops." He remained a lifelong friend and champion of Pushkin. At critical moments when Pushkin clashed with the government he used his high connections at the Court to intercede for the poet and later, after his death, to aid his family.

Pushkin may not always have found Zhukovsky's poetry and ideas sympathetic, but he admired his "captivating sweetness" and learned from his great craftsmanship. All his life he loyally defended his friend against any public criticism, mindful, no doubt, of all Zhukovsky had done to help him. On 25 January 1825, he wrote to Kondratii Ryleev: "I do not quite agree with [Bestuzhev's] stern sentence against Zhukovsky. Why should we bite the breasts of our wet nurse? Because we have cut our teeth? Say what you will, Zhukovsky has had a decisive influence on the spirit of our literature; moreover, his style of translation will forever remain the model. Oh! there's the republic of letters for you. Why does it condemn, why does it crown with laurels?" And on 25 May 1825, he mildly chastized Viazemsky: "But you are too protective of me with regard to Zhukovsky. I am not his successor, but precisely his disciple, and I succeed only in that I do not presume to push onto his highway, but wander on a country road!"

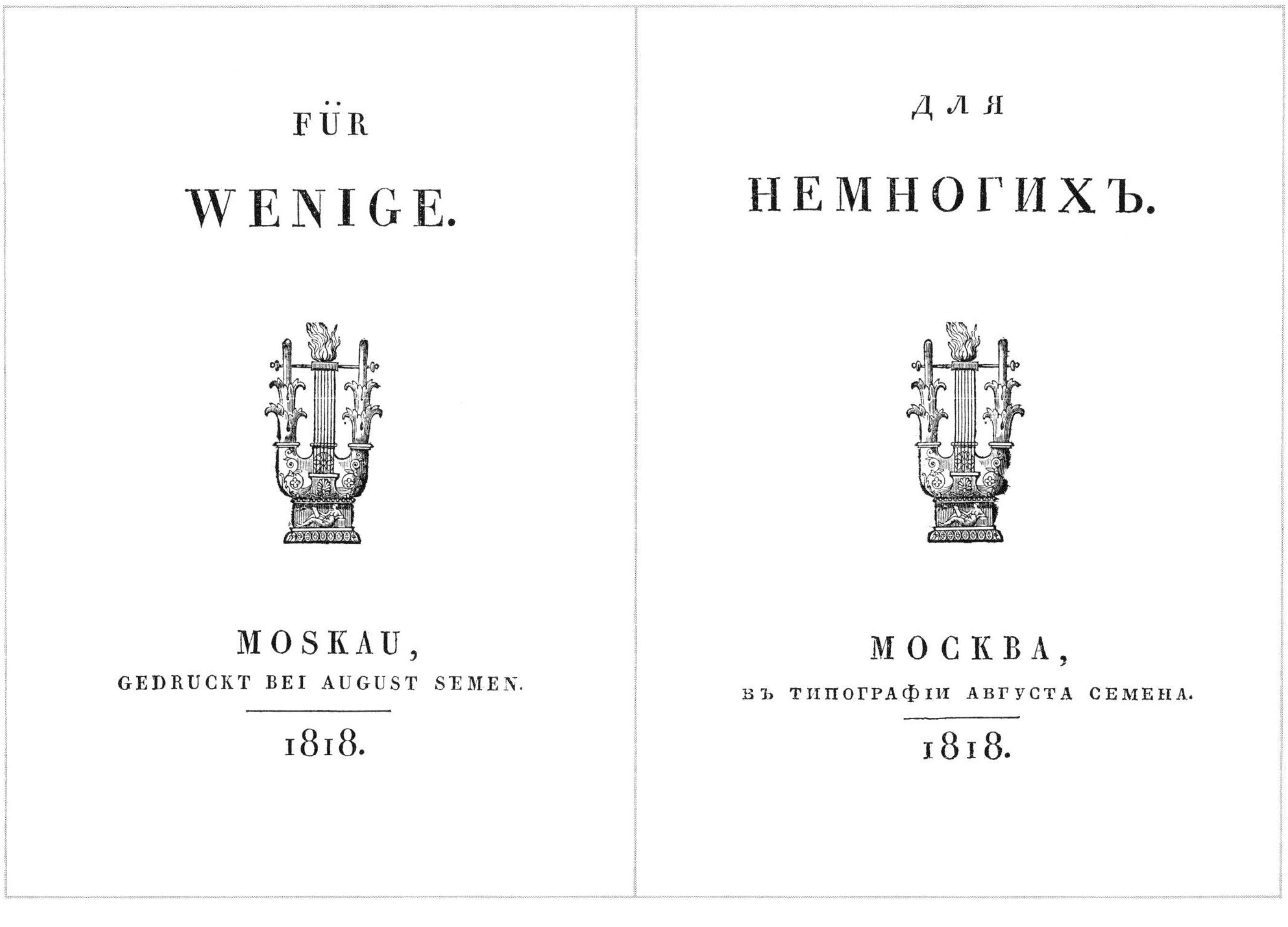

FÜR

WENIGE.

MOSKAU,
GEDRUCKT BEI AUGUST SEMEN.

1818.

ДЛЯ

НЕМНОГИХЪ.

МОСКВА,
ВЪ ТИПОГРАФІИ АВГУСТА СЕМЕНА.

1818.

In 1817, Zhukovsky was appointed Russian tutor to the Prussian princess Frederika Louisa Charlotta Wilhelmina (1798–1860), daughter of King Frederick William III. She took the name Alexandra Fedorovna when she converted to Orthodoxy upon her marriage to Grand Duke Nicholas, the future Nicholas I. The six issues of *Für Wenige*, published anonymously between January-June 1818, were intended for Zhukovsky's lessons with his royal pupil, who learned by heart his Russian translations of the German and French lyrics (none of whose authors are identified) printed on the left facing the Russian texts. Zhukovsky included some of his most famous translations, or, more accurately, adaptations, of Uhland, Goethe ("Mignon," "Der Erlkönig"), Schiller, Hebel, and others in the little volumes, and his rendering of Schiller's dramatic poem *Die Jungfrau von Orleans (Orleanskaia deva)* appeared for the first time in No. VI (without the German original), taking up the entire issue.

This important example of an entirely private publication, which circulated only among Zhukovsky's closest friends and in an intimate circle connected with the Imperial court, is typical of the decade, when the elite of Russian letters was far better known to itself than to the outside world, and when many poets had reputations founded exclusively on unpublished works. As Pushkin remarked in an April 1820 letter to Viazemsky: "The circle of poets is becoming tighter hour by hour — soon we shall be forced, for lack of listeners, to read our verses aloud to each other. And that's not so bad."

6

Nikolai Ivanovich Gnedich (1784-1833) *translator*, The Iliad of Homer.

***Iliada Gomera*. 2 pts. St. Petersburg, 1829.**

Kilgour 337

Gnedich, a well-educated poet and translator of Ukrainian origin, fluent in several languages, devoted over two decades of his adult life to translating the *Iliad*, which Russians like Pushkin primarily knew through the twelve-volume French adaptation of P. J. Bitaubé (1787–88). In 1807 he thought only of continuing Kostrov's unfinished rendering in Alexandrines, but by 1811 he had decided to begin his own version in hexameters. He published the first fragments in 1813, and from then on Russian literary and offical society anxiously followed the course of his labor. The government, recognizing the significance of the undertaking, effectively subsidized the project when it awarded him a well-paid sinecure in the Imperial Public Library in Petersburg. In addition he received an annual pension of 1,500 rubles from March 1825 on. Pushkin envied, but did not begrudge this kind of enlightened "literary encouragement," as he made clear when he wrote to Aleksandr Bestuzhev: "The age of Catherine is the age of encouragement; that does not make it inferior to any other. Karamzin, it seems, is encouraged; Zhukovsky cannot complain, nor Krylov either. Gnedich is completing his heroic feat in the quiet of his study; we shall see when his Homer will appear" (end of May/beginning of June 1825). During the years of his exile from Russia's capitals, Pushkin often enquired after Gnedich's progress in letters to Gnedich himself and other friends.

Shortly after the Imperial Academy of Sciences issued the two volumes in December 1829, Pushkin saluted Gnedich's achievement in an unsigned note in *The Literary Gazette* (No. 2, 1830): "The translation of the *Iliad*, so long and so impatiently awaited, has at last appeared! When writers, spoiled by fleeting successes, have for the most part concentrated on brilliant trifles, when talent shuns work, while fashion scorns the models of majestic antiquity, when poetry is not reverent service, but merely a frivolous pastime, we regard with a feeling of deep respect and gratitude a poet who has proudly dedicated the best years of his life to one labor alone, to disinterested inspiration, and to the completion of a single, sublime heroic feat. The Russian *Iliad* is before us. We turn to studying it so that in time we may give an account to our readers of a book which is bound to have such an important influence on our native literature." Gnedich's remains the standard Russian verse translation.

Part One is open to the beginning of the First Book and a vignette by the popular engraver Nikolai Ivanovich Utkin (1780–1863) representing the heads of seven heroes of the Trojan War, identified in a note on page xvi as, from left to right, Agamemnon, Achilleus, Nestor, Odysseus, Diomedes, Paris, and Menelaos. Part Two (not shown) includes a fold-out map of Troy with a detailed rendering of the disposition of the Greek forces.

7

Volkonskaia poetry album.

No fashionable Russian home in Pushkin's day considered itself cultivated unless the owners could boast of an album in which guests, both distinguished (preferably) and little known, had inscribed poems in honor of their hosts, salutations, drawings, a few bars of music, and other mementos of their visit. The salon of Princess Zinaida Aleksandrovna Volkonskaia (1792–1862), a famous beauty dubbed by her contemporaries "the Northern Corinne" (after the heroine of Mme. de Staël's 1807 novel *Corinne*) because of her many talents, was among Moscow's most prominent in the years 1824–29. Writers like Viazemsky, Del'vig, Zhukovsky, Mickiewicz, and Venevitinov frequented the house of this hostess who helped shape the great age of familiar literary associations. She was both a composer and a singer; Rossini praised her musical appearances in Paris in 1815. Pushkin, too, attended the gatherings and concerts she organized. He called her "the empress of the Muses and of beauty" in "To Princess Z. A. Volkonskaia, on sending her the poem 'The Gypsies'," and presented her a holograph manuscript copy of his 1827 poem "*Sredi rasseiannoi Moskvy . . .* " ("Midst dissipated Moscow . . . ", dated 6 May 1827; in the Kilgour collection).

In February 1829, she left Russia for good and settled in Rome, taking with her several albums (of verse, letters, drawings) which are now part of her literary papers in the Kilgour collection. On display here is her poetry album, with verse in French and Italian, and various writings in Russian by Viazemsky, Baratynsky, Kozlov, Venevitinov, Shevyrev, Ivan Kireevsky, Odoevsky, and others. It is open to Baratynsky's affecting "*Iz tsarstva vista i zimy . . .* " ("From the kingdom of whist and winter . . ."), signed "Moscow. 26 January 1829, on the occasion of the departure of P[rincess] Z[inaida] A[leksandrovna] V[olkonsk]aia," which he published later that year in *The Snowdrop for 1829* as "To Princess Z. A. Volkonskaia on her departure for Italy" (" . . . So, the idol of our heart, we sadly see her off to a better land and a better world"). The autograph differs from the text in standard modern editions both in several textual points and in matters of punctuation.

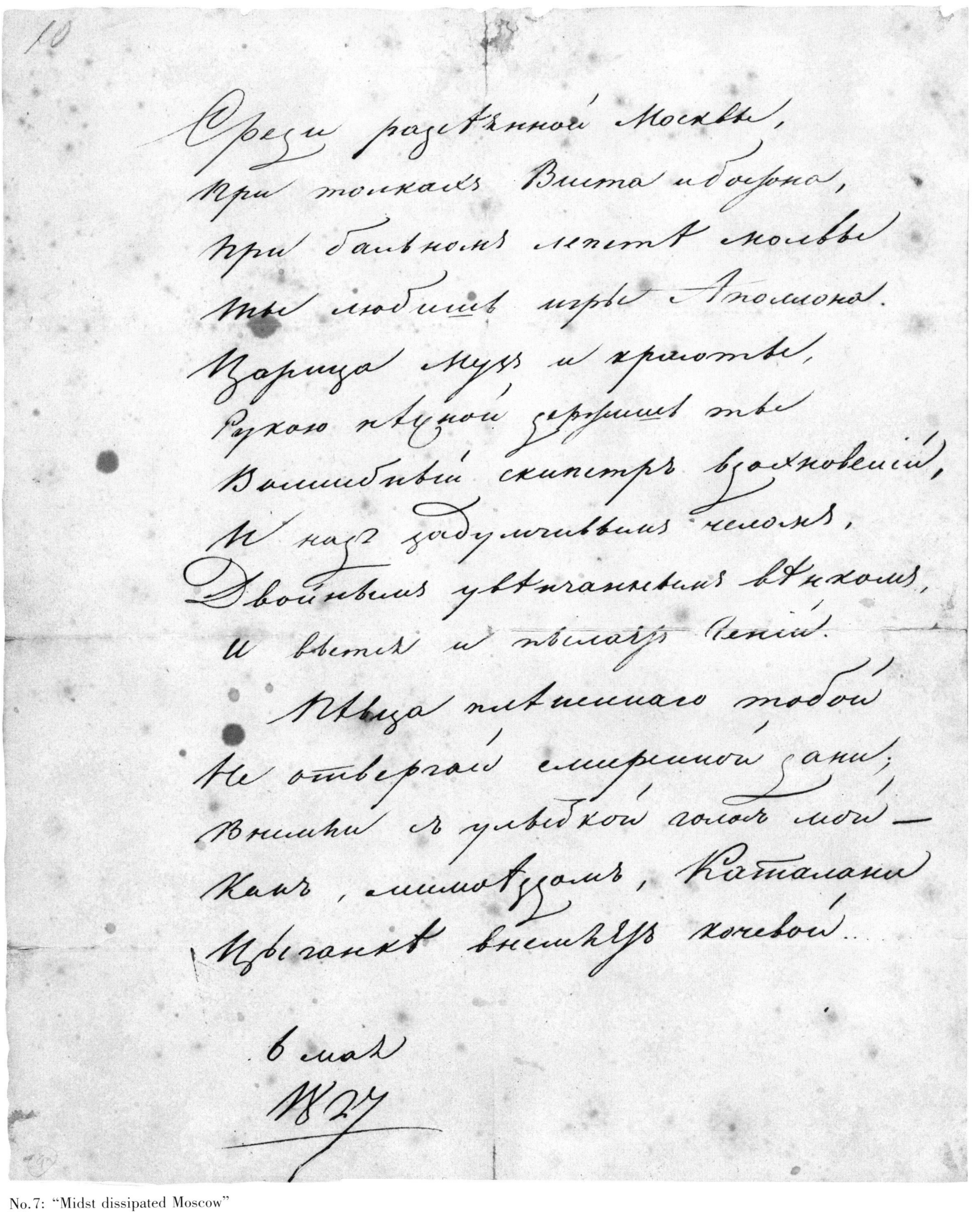

10

Среди разсѣянной Москвы,
При толкахъ Виста и бостона,
При бальномъ лепетѣ молвы
Ты любишь игры Аполлона.
Царица Музъ и красоты,
Рукою нѣжной держишь ты
Волшебный скиптръ вдохновеній,
И надъ задумчивымъ челомъ,
Двойнымъ увѣнчаннымъ вѣнкомъ,
И вьется и пылаетъ Геній.
Пѣвца плѣненнаго тобой
Не отвергай смиренной дани;
Внемли съ улыбкой голосъ мой —
Какъ, мимоѣздомъ, Каталани
Цыганкѣ внемлетъ кочевой...

6 мая
1827

No.7: "Midst dissipated Moscow"

Two volumes of unpublished letters and literary texts from the Volkonskaia archive, edited by Dr. Bayara Aroutunova with commentaries and analysis, are scheduled to appear in 1987–88.

8

Evgenii Abramovich Baratynsky (1800-44), The Concubine.

***Nalozhnitsa.* Moscow, 1831.**

Kilgour 102

Until 1828 no copyright laws existed in Russia and no writer's text was protected from unauthorized publication or mutilation. Unscrupulous publishers pirated both printed and unprinted manuscripts, particularly the latter, as so many works circulated in copies among an author's friends and acquaintances that they could easily pass into other hands. The 1828 law did not put full stop to the practice. The copy of *The Concubine* on display here is open to the author's signature on verso of the title-page, under the printed statement: "All copies of this book, not

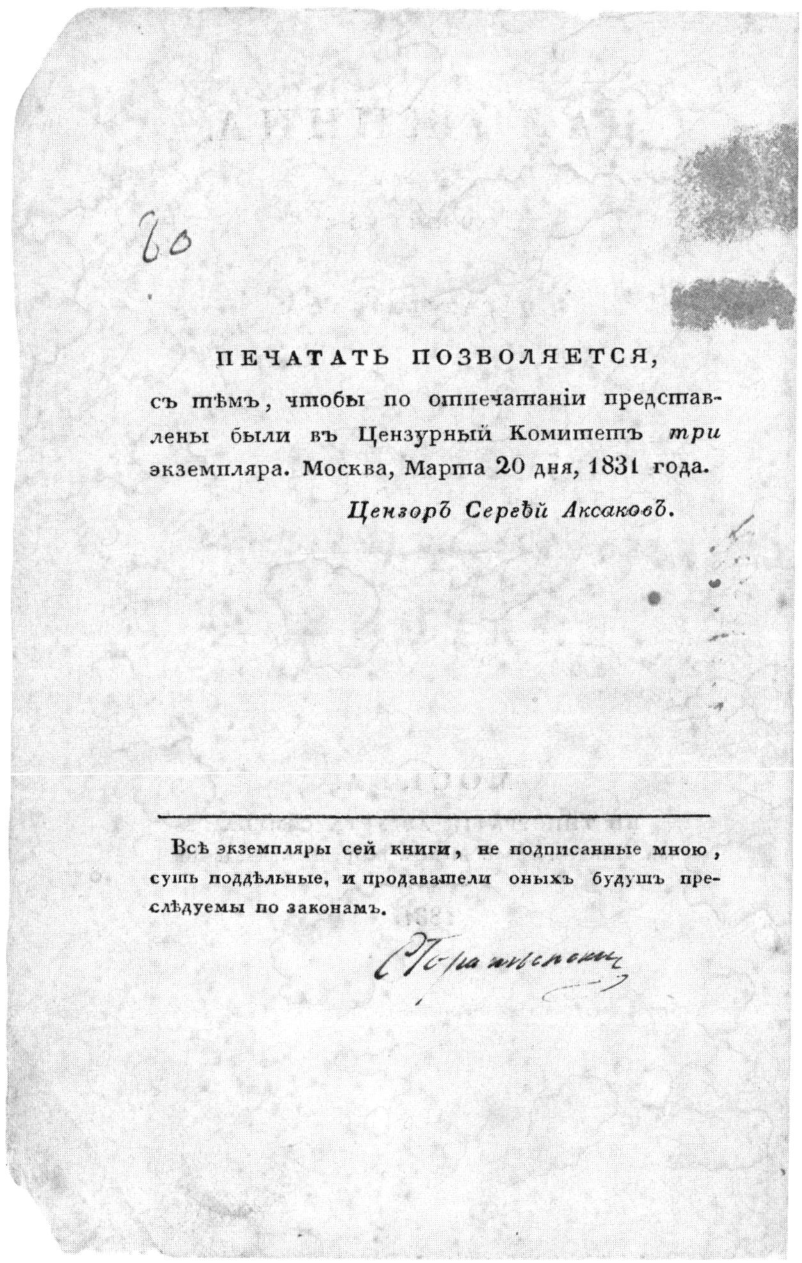

ПЕЧАТАТЬ ПОЗВОЛЯЕТСЯ,

съ тѣмъ, чтобы по отпечатаніи представлены были въ Цензурный Комитетъ *три* экземпляра. Москва, Марта 20 дня, 1831 года.

Ценсоръ Сергѣй Аксаковъ.

Всѣ экземпляры сей книги, не подписанные мною, суть поддѣльные, и продаватели оныхъ будутъ преслѣдуемы по законамъ.

signed by me, are forgeries, and those who sell them will be prosecuted according to the laws." The censor for the book, passed on 20 March 1831, was the novelist-memoirist Sergei Aksakov (1791–1859), author of *A Family Chronicle and The Childhood Years of Bagrov-Grandson.*

In a letter of 7 January 1831 to Petr Pletnev, Pushkin called the work "a marvel." Baratynsky renamed the long poem *Tsyganka (The Gypsy Girl)* when he published the final text in his 1835 collected verse.

9

Aleksandr Anfimovich Orlov (ca. 1790-1840), The Devil's Nights, or A New Do not listen, if you don't like it, but let me tell lies.

Chortovy nochi, ili, Novoe Ne liubo, ne slushai, a lgat' ne meshai. **7 pts.**
Moscow, 1833.

Kilgour 803

Orlov, a tireless scribbler and enterprising pulp *littérateur (lubochnii pisatel')*, produced countless chapbooks and songbooks in the 1820's and 1830's, but he was most popular for his sequels to previously published works of others (such as his seven imitations of Bulgarin's *Ivan Vyzhigin*) or himself (six "Nights" followed the "First Night" of the book on display here, which bears the bookplate of A. Smirdin's circulating library, No. 16403). Pushkin ignored Orlov's pirating of his own works (lyrics and narrative poems) in cheap, mass-produced pamphlets aimed at a semi-literate audience. Pushkin did not, however, ignore it when his copyright was infringed upon by publishers for the more exclusive public.

Orlov has a more than modest place in literary history (and in this exhibition) only for the minor role he played in one of Pushkin's most famous attacks on Faddei Bulgarin, his chief critical adversary in the 1830's. In the pseudonymous critical essay "The Triumph of Friendship, or the Vindicated Aleksandr Anfimovich Orlov" (signed "Feofilakt Kosichkin", when published in *Telescope*, No. 13, 1831) Pushkin savagely compared Bulgarin, the self-styled "gentleman writer," with the hapless chapbook novelist. Both have something to sell: the poor but honest Orlov his sequels, Bulgarin his honor and credibility. Commerce alone motivates both, but with different degrees of honesty. Poor Orlov took Pushkin's ironic "defense" entirely seriously, and wrote to thank him. This prompted a tongue-in-cheek response from Pushkin on 24 November 1831: "I rejoice that my defense, within my poor powers, of a talent which, of course, has no need of any defense, has earned your favor. . . . The first chapter of your new Vyzhigin is new proof of the inexhaustibility of your talent. But honored Aleksandr Anfimovich, restrain this noble, just indignation, curb the ferocity of your creative spirit!"

10

Lubki **(Russian broadsides with woodcut illustrations).**

Prince Petr Andreevich Viazemsky (1792–1878), ***Troika.*** **[n.p., 1854?]**

Kilgour 1253 (3 pieces)

The Kilgour collection contains a fine group of these popular folk prints, most dating from the mid- to late nineteenth century. Shown here are two which demonstrate the uses (and abuses) of the folk medium by popular and high culture alike.

Aleksei Vasil'evich Koltsov (1809–42), the first in a series of so-called "peasant poets" (although as the son of a wealthy cattle dealer he can hardly be considered a peasant), enjoyed a modest fame for his popular songs and other folk-style lyrics on peasant subjects. In 1835, Belinsky and Stankevich brought out the first collection of the verse of this largely self-taught poet. Pushkin was interested enough in his poetry to publish him in *The Contemporary* in 1836. His folk-inspired "*Chto ty spish' muzhichek, / Ved' vesna na dvore . . .* " ("Muzhik, what are you sleeping for? It's already spring outside . . . ") of 1839 first appeared in *The Notes of the Fatherland*, vol. XIV (1841) and was immediately pirated for *lubki*. In some cases, as in the example shown here, the "publisher" simply printed the text of the poem (without any attribution or date) with an appropriate illustration. In several other instances, *lubki* on its theme of the lazy peasant were prepared using only snatches of the poem itself.

Нов

Вотъ мчится тройка удалая. или Вотъ какъ мужь

Вотъ тройка мчится удалая,
Клубится снегъ подъ ней сталбомъ.
Въ карню Ѳитинья молодая
Такъ мило жмется подъ кнутомъ.
Афимья лѣвая пристяжка,
Бѣжитъ съ поникшій головой,
А съ права помогаетъ Дашка
Разиня страшно ротикъ свой.
И тройкой трое управляютъ
Иванъ Антипъ и Пантелей,
Немилосердно женъ хлестаютъ
И правятъ всякой самъ своей.

За что жъ такъ женужки тру
Зачто, такъ жмутся отъ кну
Зачто мужья нанихъ сердя
Какая есть нанихъ вина
Ѳитинья модѣ подражала
Лошадокъ мужъ ея продал
Она наславу щеголяла,
Теперя жъ мужъ ее взну
Афимья Ѳомку полюбила
У мужа деньги унесла
И всѣ съ дружечкомъ прок
Зато вч пристяжку теперь ш

…НЯ

…справляютъ, Отъ глупостей отучаютъ.

…ка сладко ѣсть умѣла,
…изна страшно такъ была,
…пироги да кашу ѣла
…о теперя слѣва шла.
…ья ужъ дѣлать что незнали
…мали женъ усмирить
…льно шипко такъ хлистали
…и ихъ какъ въ свѣтѣ жить.
…инья моду забываетъ,
…мьи, Ѳомка ужъ постылъ,
…ь сладко Дашка отвыкаетъ,
…ъ такъ тягостенъ имъ былъ.

Смотрите ужъ они стонаютъ,
Мужей милушками завутъ,
Простить ихъ сильно убѣждаютъ
Горючи Слезы токомъ льютъ.
Мужья прастить ихъ согласились
Вернули тройку вмигъ назадъ
Ихъ жены страшно веселились
И изъ мужей былъ всякой радъ.
Ивотъ назадъ тройка катаетъ.
Покорность стала въ ней видна
Се кнутъ болѣ нехлистаетъ.
Она ужъ сдѣлалась смирна.–

183

No. 10:
"A new song . . ."

The second *lubok* shown illustrates an altogether more curious and complex interaction between the popular and high cultures. Fedor Nikolaevich Glinka (1786–1880), cousin of the composer, wrote verse on a wide range of subjects. His religious verse, some gathered in the 1826 *Opyty sviashchennoi poezii* (also in the Kilgour collection) probably represents his finest achievement as a poet, but he is most famous for his songs in the folk style, especially for the 1824 "Troika." He borrowed its opening lines from a folk song, but it was his adaptation which spread the popularity of the "troika theme" throughout Russian culture.

The undated *lubok* on display here, entitled "Novaia *pesnia. Vot mchitsia troika udalaia ili Vot kak muzh'ia zhen ispravliaiut, ot glupostei otuchaiut*" ("A *New* Song. There races the dashing troika, or Here's how husbands reform their wives and break them of stupidities") uses the song's first line only for a sexist parody of its subject.

Prince Petr Viazemsky, one of Pushkin's closest friends and favorite correspondents, borrows both opening lines of Glinka's poem for his own variation on the theme. The poem, written in celebration of a Russian victory on 23 March 1854 in the Danubian campaign against Turkey, reflects his increasing conservatism and chauvinism, which had been provoked by the revolutionary outbreaks of 1848, when he penned his famous "*Sviataia Rus'* " ("Holy Russia", also in the Kilgour collection). Viewed as a dangerous liberal by Nicholas I, Viazemsky was close to the family of his son, Alexander II, and the undated "Troika" (there is no title and only "Prince Viazemsky" at the end) is contained in a portfolio with the bookplate of the Emperor, to whom this copy was probably presented. The poem does not appear in standard Soviet editions of Viazemsky's works.

· II ·

PRECURSORS OF THE EARLY LYRICS

One of the central literary issues of Pushkin's youth involved the figure of the author. Each of the ways of life, or institutions, that was illustrated by the texts in the previous case provided an authorial role: the anonymous scribe of the chapbook trade, the familiar interlocutor of the salons and literary circles, the dutiful subject and wise preceptor-scholar who found favor with the Imperial patron. But these roles became realized in the poetry of Pushkin's youth in many ways. Just as a good salon conversationalist, an *honnête homme*, was expected to converse as a non-specialist on a variety of topics, a poet who worked in this milieu of the educated, Westernized gentry was expected to practice a variety of genres, each of which tended to express a certain feeling: patriotic fervor in odes, melancholy in elegies, trenchant wit in epigrams, or righteous indignation in satires.

Nevertheless, few poets except Pushkin could excel in all genres, and a poet generally acquired an authorial image from the persona of the genre or genres in which he or she gained the attention of the readers and listeners of the time. To have such an image, however, was not yet to have a developed biography, as the poets of the Romantic age, following Byron, would come to acquire. Poetic anthologies such as Nikol'sky's, were organized by genres, as a rule, and not (as in more recent times) by the works of individual poets, arranged chronologically. Even the collected works of an individual poet, tended, like Batiushkov's in this case, to follow the generic pattern. Yet the relative paucity of categories in Batiushkov's *Essays in Verse* ("elegies," "epistles," "miscellaneous") suggests that such categories were beginning to yield to the more general sense of a lyric poem that would characterize the Romantic period, in turn leaving a space for the image of the poet to acquire a life history, which had not yet been constituted in the literature of Pushkin's youth.

The materials in this case include texts that helped create authorial images for the best known of Pushkin's senior contemporaries: Krylov, the crafty fabulist; Derzhavin, the independent devotee of friendship, rural life, and simple delights; Zhukovsky, who celebrated the Russian campaign against the French from the perspective of officers and men, not the Autocrat; Batiushkov, who was the major theoretician and poetic craftsman of the "light verse" that the first two decades of the century treasured. Derzhavin's ode plays a discordant note among these manifestations of noble independence from the court poetry of the eighteenth century, an odic tradition that Derzhavin himself had done much to undermine with his conversational "Ode to Felitsa" (1782) and with the *Anacreontic Songs* displayed here. It is perhaps not accidental, given recent developments in Soviet society and culture, that Derzhavin's *Anacreontic Songs* have just been reprinted in a handsome edition (1986).

W M T

11

Pavel Aleksandrovich Nikol'sky (1790-1816), *editor*, The Pantheon of Russian poetry.

***Panteon russkoi poezii.* 6 v. St. Petersburg, 1814.**

Kilgour 816

In the preface to this popular anthology, printed by the Imperial Academy of Sciences in three parts (each part in two books), Nikol'sky offered his "pleasant and useful book" to the public in the hope that it might "be of use to lovers of literature." He called the plan of his collection "entirely new." The organization of each part, however, in the following order clearly reflects the reigning genre hierarchy which, while already challenged, would rule for at least a decade longer: "Spiritual, Solemn, Moral and Anacreontic Odes; Epistles; Satires; Elegies; Idylls; Tales and Stories; Fables; Songs and Romances; Epigrams, Madrigals and Inscriptions; and finally Excerpts from Narrative Poems, Tragedies and Comedies." The collection contains works of writers like Lomonosov, Derzhavin, Kapnist, Karamzin, and Dmitriev who had already achieved "classic" status, and works, in many instances first publications, by Krylov, Zhukovsky, Viazemsky, Batiushkov, and many others now footnotes in literary history. There is a Pushkin represented too, but it is "our" poet's paternal uncle, well enough known to require no initials. No authors are identified in the table of contents, but individual works are at least signed with the author's name, an innovatory practice for the time.

12

V. A. Zhukovsky, A bard in the camp of Russian warriors.

***Pevets Vo stane ruskikh voinov.* St. Petersburg, 1813.**

Diaghilev-Lifar library 815

In 1812, with the onset of the French invasion of Russia, Zhukovsky, already well-known in the small circle of Russian writers for his free translation of Gray's "A Country Churchyard," Bürger's "Lenore" ("Liudmila"), and for his scrupulous editing of *The Messenger of Europe* (1808–10), enlisted in the Moscow militia. He witnessed the battle of Borodino (his reserve unit took no part in the action), and wrote "A Bard" (or "The Warrior's Goblet," as he first called it) while attached to the staff headquarters of the Russian army, which was pursuing and harassing the retreating French. As the work progressed, he read it to officers on the staff. They promptly copied its first, variant text and spread it throughout the army, where it was quickly committed to memory. The fresh style of form and language and its extolling not only of the Tsar and his generals, but of the friendship among the officers and common soldiers stood in striking contrast to the tradition of the Russian military odes of the eighteenth century, which enjoyed a populous but sterile revival (Derzhavin's "Ode on the Reception of the Victor," for example) during the "patriotic war" with Napoleon's France.

Zhukovsky's friends, who for many years referred to him simply as "the Bard," hailed the work as a masterpiece. Pushkin's uncle, Vasilii L'vovich, pronounced it "the finest work in the Russian language" in a letter to Viazemsky, while Batiushkov saluted Zhukovsky for having "done wonders with the lyre, if not with the sword. . . . Thank God the bullets flew by you [at Borodino]! Phoebus himself saved you." Many years later, in an unfinished article of 1830 ("An Experiment in Replying to Several Non-literary Accusations"), Pushkin would single out the work: "Just as our literature can with pride display before Europe Karamzin's *History*, a few odes, a few fables, Zhukovsky's paean of the year 1812, a translation of the *Iliad*, a few flowers of elegiac poetry, so our criticism can show a few separate articles. . . ."

A Bard in the Camp of Russian Warriors, Zhukovsky's first separate publication, appeared in January 1813. This heroic elegy-ode and the two-volume collected *Stikhotvoreniia* (Poems, 1815–16; also in the Kilgour collection) sealed Zhukovsky's popularity and prestige (in 1816 he was awarded an annual pension of 4,000 rubles), and insured his influence on the young for a generation.

By an ironic turn of fate the Kilgour copy was in the past bound with an "imitation of [Edward] Young" entitled *Noch' na grobakh* (St. Petersburg, 1812) by Prince S. A. Shirinsky-Shikhmatov (1783–1837), whom Pushkin called a "soulless, cold, inflated, boring windbag." Zhukovsky thus finds himself between two

covers with one of the most prominent members of Admiral A. S. Shishkov's Colloquium of Lovers of the Russian Word, which excoriated everything that he and his friends in the rival Arzamas circle stood for in literature.

13

Gavrila Romanovich Derzhavin (1743–1816), Ode on the reception of the victor . . . Alexander the First.

Oda na sretenie pobeditelia, svoboditelia i primiritelia Evropy, velikogo i svyshe blagoslovlennogo Imperatora otsa otechestva Aleksandra pervogo.
St. Petersburg, [1814].

Kilgour 266

Pushkin's attitude to Derzhavin, "Russia's first outstanding poet" (Nabokov) and a kind of elder statesman of Russian letters by the time of Pushkin's youth, wavered between praise for his rough touches of genius and denigration of his incorrectness of language and uneven style. We sometimes find swings of opinion even within the space of one document. So, in a letter to Aleksandr Bestuzhev (end of May/beginning of June 1825), Pushkin could call him and Krylov the only geniuses of Russian literature and rank him "as much above J. B. Rousseau" as Krylov was above La Fontaine. Yet a few lines earlier he had assayed his "idol" as "$\frac{1}{4}$ gold and $\frac{3}{4}$ lead." A week or so later, between 1 and 8 June, he wrote to Del'vig: "After your departure I reread all of Derzhavin, and here is my final opinion. That eccentric knew neither the Russian ABC's nor the spirit of the Russian language (and that is why he is inferior to Lomonosov). He had no conception either of style or harmony—or even of the rules of versification. That is why he must infuriate every discriminating ear. He not only does not sustain an *ode*, but he cannot sustain even a stanza (you know the exceptions). What then is in him: *thoughts, pictures, and truly poetic impulses*; reading him, you seem to be reading a bad, free translation of some marvelous original. I swear his genius thought in Tartar—but he did not know the Russian ABC's from lack of leisure [to learn them]. Derzhavin, when he has in due course been translated, will astonish Europe, and out of national pride we shall not say everything we know about him (to say nothing of his ministry [Derzhavin was Minister of Justice from 1802–03]). Some eight odes and several fragments of Derzhavin's will have to be preserved, but burn the rest."

When Pushkin summed up his verdict on Derzhavin to Del'vig he may well have had in mind the leaden patriotic odes that the aged poet wrote during and after the War of 1812. Pushkin parodied their archaic diction (requiring a footnote for one word in the second line of the ode displayed here) and clumsy, convoluted style in his satirical poem "Fonvizin's Shade" (November-December 1815). Pushkin portrays the shade of the satirist Denis Fonvizin (1745–92) hearing Derzhavin read one of his late odes and sighing "What has happened to you, Derzhavin?" and he himself exclaims: "Denis! he [Derzhavin] will always be famous, / But, O why should one live so long!"

The date of this ode, left blank on the title page, was probably 26 July 1814, the first after Alexander's arrival in the capital to be set aside for public ceremonies. The folio volume is open to one of two allegorical vignettes, this one portraying, as a note explains, "Apollo, having killed the Python, . . . enters a triumphal gate on which is the inscription: To the Victor and Peacemaker."

14

G. R. Derzhavin, Anacreontic songs.

Anakreonticheskie pesni.
St. Petersburg, 1804.

Kilgour 265

Pushkin had no reservations about the significance of Derzhavin's anacreontic verse, the culmination of a half-century of the genre's evolution and one of his last great works before what Pushkin and his friends considered the onset of senility. Pushkin recognized its important contribution to the "light poetry" of his youth, and as late as 1830, in "Refutation of Criticism," wrote *à propos* his own *Count Nulin*: "And the erotic poems of Derzhavin — innocent, great Derzhavin? But laying aside in-

Я сердцами обю челомъ.

equality in poetic merit, *Count Nulin* must yield to them, both in the freedom and in the vivacity of the jokes."

Pushkin was copying out the final text of Chapter Eight of *Eugene Onegin* at the same time as he worked on the "Refutation" at Boldino in the autumn of 1830. Lines 3 – 4 of the second stanza of Chapter Eight — "The aged Derzhavin noticed us — and blessed us / As he descended to the grave" — recall Pushkin's one encounter with the poet, which he later (1835) set down in a charming if not entirely accurate account:

> I saw Derzhavin only once in my life, but I shall never forget the occasion. It was in 1815, at a public examination in the Lycée. When we learned that Derzhavin was coming, we all grew excited. Del'vig went out on the stairs to wait for him and to kiss his hand, the hand that had written "The Waterfall." Derzhavin arrived. He entered the vestibule, and Del'vig heard him ask the door-keeper: "Where's the privy, my good fellow?" This prosaic question disenchanted Del'vig, who gave up his intention and returned to

the hall. Del'vig told me the story with wonderful bonhomie and good humor. Derzhavin was very old. He was wearing a uniform and velveteen boots. Our examination fatigued him. He sat with his head propped on one hand. His expression was inane, his eyes dull, his lip drooped; his portrait (where he is shown in a nightcap and dressing gown) is a very good likeness. He dozed until the examination in Russian literature began. Then he came to life, his eyes began sparkling; he was completely transformed. Of course, his poems were being read, his poems analyzed, his poems that were praised every minute. He listened with extraordinary animation. At last I was called. I recited my "Recollections at Tsarskoe Selo" while standing but a few steps from Derzhavin. I am powerless to describe the state of my Soul: when I reached the line where I mention Derzhavin's name, my youthful voice vibrated and my heart throbbed with intoxicating rapture. . . . I do not remember how I finished my recitation; I do not remember where I fled. Derzhavin was thoroughly delighted; he demanded my presence, he wanted to embrace me. . . . They looked for me, but did not find me.

15

Konstantin Nikolaevich Batiushkov (1787–1855), Essays in verse and prose.

***Opyty v stikhakh i proze*. 2 v. St. Petersburg, 1817.**

Kilgour 108

This gentleman-poet of genius, the well-educated nephew of Karamzin's protector, M. N. Murav'ev, served with distinction in the Russian campaigns against France, and then as a diplomat to the Bourbon court in Naples. He loved the culture of Italy, especially its Renaissance masters Petrarch and Tasso, and tried with remarkable success to make his native language "sing" with the same mellifluousness as Italian (Pushkin in 1824 commented that "Batiushkov, Lomonosov's fortunate successor, did for the Russian language what Petrarch did for Italian.") He gathered his finest works into the two-volume *Essays*, which Gnedich published, making a windfall profit of 13,000 rubles for himself (he turned over a mere 2,000 rubles to the poet). Pushkin's early diction came equally under the spell of Zhukovsky and Batiushkov, especially the latter's sensuous concreteness.

In 1822 Batiushkov attempted to take his own life; madness clouded the last three decades of his life. On 25 January 1825, Pushkin wrote to Ryleev: "As regards Batiushkov, let us esteem in him the misfortunes and the unrealized hopes." Sometime in the 1830's he paid the poet the highest compliment of carefully rereading the *Essays* and making extensive marginal comments, critical but respectful and often very admiring.

16

Ivan Andreevich Krylov (1768 or 1769–1844), Fables.

***Basni*. St. Petersburg, 1809.**

———. 2 pts. St. Petersburg, 1834.

Kilgour 569 & 576

Krylov, a rather déclassé member of the lower gentry and cardsharp, but a talented journalist and playwright, achieved sudden fame with the publication in 1809 of the first book of his collected fables. Financial security followed quickly, when the government granted him a sinecure at the Imperial Public Library in 1810. Book after book of fables, written in free iambics and an earthy, colloquial Russian, secured his position as Russia's greatest fabulist.

In his letters, Pushkin placed Krylov's achievement above that of La Fontaine, although he played the diplomat in his 1825 review of a Paris collection of French and Italian translations of Krylov's fables sponsored by Count G. V. Orlov ("On Monsieur Lémontey's Introduction to the Translation of I. A. Krylov's *Fables*"): "In conclusion I will say that we must thank Count Orlov for choosing a truly national poet to introduce Europe to the literature of the North. Of course no Frenchman

ОПЫТЫ

ВЪ СТИХАХЪ И ПРОЗѢ

К. Батюшкова.

ВЪ С. ПЕТЕРБУРГѢ

1817.

ОПЫТЫ

ВЪ СТИХАХЪ И ПРОЗѢ

К. Батюшкова.

ВЪ С. ПЕТЕРБУРГѢ

1817.

No. 15

would dare to place anyone at all above La Fontaine, but we, I think, may be allowed to prefer Krylov. Both of them will forever remain their countrymen's favorites. Someone has justly remarked that simplicity (*naïveté, bonhomie*) is the innate attribute of the French people; in contrast, the distinctive trait of our ways is a certain gay slyness of mind, a spirit of mockery, and a vivid way of expressing ourselves. La Fontaine and Krylov are representatives of the spirit of both their peoples." Viazemsky's objections to Pushkin's article prompted a typically irreverent reply: "Your criticism of Krylov is killingly on the mark; be quiet, I know it myself, but that rat is an old crony of mine. I called him a representative of the *spirit* of the Russian people — I don't vouch that it doesn't stink in some respects. In days of old our common people were called smerd [stench] (cf. Mr. Karamzin). The point is that Krylov is a most original carcass, Count Orlov is a fool, but we're all scatterbrains, etc., etc." (about 7 November 1825).

On display are the 1809 first edition of the fables (twenty-three), with book stamp of the Imperial Library of Tsarskoe Selo, and Part Two, Book Six of the 1834 edition, published by Aleksandr Smirdin with illustrations by A. P. Sapozhnikov. The 1834 edition is open to the 1818 "*Osel i muzhik*" ("The Ass and the Bumpkin"), first published in Book Six of the 1819 edition of the *Fables* (also in the Kilgour collection). Pushkin himself heard Krylov recite it in 1819, at the

No. 16:
Krylov (from no. 58)

Petersburg mansion of the well-known patron of the arts and president of the Academy of Arts, Aleksei Olenin (1763–1843), and he deliberately echoed line four of the fable in the opening line of *Eugene Onegin*. Nabokov neatly summarizes the fable: "When told by the countryman to patrol the vegetable garden, he [the ass] did not touch a cabbage leaf; indeed, he galloped about so vigilantly that he ruined the whole place, for which he was cudgeled by its owner: asininity should not accept grave tasks, but he errs, too, who gives an ass a watchman's job."

17

Vasilii L'vovich Pushkin (1767?/70?-1830), Poems.

Stikhotvoreniia.
St. Petersburg, 1822.

Kilgour 908

Pushkin was close to few members of his family, but he and his amiable paternal uncle got on well. The "other Pushkin" was proud of his brilliant nephew and moved easily in the company of his friends, for whom he was a figure of affectionate fun. The Montaigne epigraph to his 1822 *Poems* shows the Classicist tastes of this Gallomaniac with a flair for light verse and excellent contacts in French literary circles. He is now remembered only for his racy little comic epic "*Opasnyi sosed*" ("The Dangerous Neighbor," 1811), whose disreputable hero, Buianov ("Mr. Rowdy"), Pushkin saluted in *Eugene Onegin* (Five, XXVI, 9) as his "first cousin," and who winds up as the first pretender for Tatiana's hand (Seven, XXVI, 2). It circulated widely in manuscript copies, but did not, of course, appear in the 1822 Poems, published by subscription and supervised by Pletnev, to whom Pushkin wrote on 9 September 1830: "Poor Uncle Vasilii! Do you know what his last words were? I came to him, found him unconscious, he came to, he recognized me, wept a little, then fell silent: '*How dull Katenin's articles are!*' and not another word. Well, what do you think of that? That's what it means to die like a trooper, on your shield, *le cri de guerre à la bouche!*"

The frontispiece portrait to which the volume is open is engraved by Stepan Galaktionov (1779–1854).

· III ·

EARLY VERSE

The materials assembled here recapitulate for Pushkin the processes of constituting a public image that attended the poets who were represented in the second case: random, unremunerated publication of works in a variety of different genres in anthologies and almanacs, followed (for serious, successful, or vain poets) by a collection whose printing was arranged and supervised by a friend. Pushkin surpassed his contemporaries not only in the brilliance and variety of his verse, but in the rapidity with which he could imagine publishing his own collected lyrics and in the casualness with which he treated them, even to losing a manuscript in a card game. As with his contemporaries, however, the collection was organized by genres (thereby demonstrating the range of his talent and sensibility), not by chronology. The chronological ordering that might have permitted contemporaries to measure the growth of the poet's mind came only with Pushkin's last lifetime collections and with his thematization of the maturing process in *Eugene Onegin*.

These editions of Pushkin's collected poems helped earn him the epithet "protean," fixed upon him, among others, by Gnedich. Its appropriateness becomes even more apparent when one recalls that not only was Pushkin writing volumes of superb lyrics during the 1820's, he was also completing much of *Eugene Onegin*, finishing his historical drama *Boris Godunov*, and beginning his first serious works in criticism and fiction. His narrative poems of the 1820's had made him Russia's most celebrated writer.

W M T

18

Aleksandr Fedorovich Voeikov (1779–1839), *editor*,
A new collection of exemplary Russian works and translations in verse, published from 1816 to 1821.

Novoe sobranie obraztsovikh ruskikh sochinenii i perevodov v stikhakh, vyshedshikh v svet ot 1816 po 1821 god. 2 pts.
St. Petersburg, 1821.

Diaghilev-Lifar library 20

On July 4th, Americans, at least those interested in Russian literature, may celebrate not one, but two occasions, their national holiday and Pushkin's first publication, the poem "*K drugu stikhotvortsu*" ("To a Friend Who Writes Verse"), signed with an anagram of his name ("Aleksandr N.k.sh.p."), in the 4 July 1814 issue of *The Messenger of Europe* (no. 13). From then on, his works, even during his six years of enforced provincial service and rustification away from Russia's capitals (1820–26), appeared in the leading literary periodicals and anthologies of the day.

In 1820, the rather unsavory literary journalist A. F. Voeikov, Professor of Russian Literature at Dorpat University and husband of Zhukovsky's cherished niece Aleksandra Andreevna, née Protasova, chose works by himself, Lomonosov, Derzhavin (these latter left out, he explained, "by mistake," from a previous edition), Dmitriev, Gnedich, Zhukovsky, Batiushkov, Viazemsky, A. F. Merzliakov, and others for inclusion in the first part of his anthology (Voeikov's name does not appear as the editor, a common practice of the time). The volume includes a fine portrait engraving of Zhukovsky by Ivan Chesky (1777-1848) opposite the title page.

The collection's second part, with an engraved portrait of Batiushkov by Orest Kiprensky (1782-1836), contains poems by many of the same authors, as well as Fedor Glinka, Davydov, Krylov, Baratynsky, and Pushkin: a fragment of *Ruslan and Liudmila*, the indifferent, but soon famous "Moldavian Song," "The Black Shawl," "The Muse" ("*V mladenchestve moem . . .* "), and the wonderful elegy "The Luminary of Day Has Gone Out . . . " ("*Pogaslo dnevnoe svetilo . . .*"), all scattered throughout the collection with no particular genre distinction (the table of contents, maddeningly enough, lists only titles, without authors' names). Pushkin's poems appeared without his knowledge or approval, as he complained in a letter to his brother and sister: "You like 'The Black Shawl'—you are right, but what a devil of a job they did of printing it" (27 July 1821, from Kishinev). Two further volumes (also in the Kilgour collection) contain "exemplary works" in prose only.

19

The Polar star : a pocket book for female and male lovers of Russian literature for 1823.

Poliarnaia zvezda : karmannaia knizhka dlia liubitel'nits i liubitelei ruskoi slovesnosti na 1823 god.

St. Petersburg, 1823.

Kilgour 850

The *Polar Star*, ably edited by the prominent political conspirators Aleksandr Bestuzhev (1797–1837) and Kondratii Ryleev (1795–1826), offered its readers an almanac's usual mix of lyric poetry, beginnings of longer works, short prose pieces, and criticism, but of such high quality that its popularity allowed the editors to take the radical step of proposing honoraria for the contributors. Almanacs had always relied on contributions from the editor's friends. The idea so upset the publisher, the bookseller Ivan Slenin (1789–1836), that in 1825 he withdrew his support and persuaded Baron Del'vig to start the rival *Northern Flowers*. In any event, the *Polar Star* would have soon come to an end, given the arrest of its two editors for their active part in the abortive Decembrist uprising.

Prose (by Bestuzhev, Bulgarin, Somov, Glinka, and others) and poetry (by Baratynsky, Viazemsky, Gnedich, Glinka, Davydov, Zhukovsky, Del'vig, Ryleev, etc.) mingle in the 1823 volume, but its table of contents is divided into two parts, Prose and Verse, within each of which authors appear alphabetically with the titles and page numbers of their works, an innovation which greatly helped readers (and future investigators). Four poems of Pushkin appeared here for the first time: "*Grechanke*" ("To a Greek Girl"), the elegy "*Uvy! zachem ona blistaet . . .*" ("Alas! why does she shine . . . ") and two works, "*Mechta voina*" ("The Warrior's Dream," best known as "Voina") and "*Ovidiiu*" ("To Ovid"), signed only with an asterisk.

Pushkin liked to identify his fate with that of another exile, Ovid, and during his 1821 stay in Bessarabia he visited, in December, several places Ovid was said to have frequented. The obvious parallels with himself in "To Ovid" ("a stern Slav, I shed no tears / But I can sympathize with yours") made Pushkin doubt that the censor would pass the poem. He suggested the following ruse when he sent his "Bessarabian ravings" to Bestuzhev on 21 June 1822: "Give my greetings to the censorship, my girlfriend of long standing; the dear old thing seems to have grown still more intelligent. I do not understand what in my elegiac fragment might trouble her chastity, however . . . . I put them completely at your disposal. I foresee obstacles in publishing my poem to Ovid, but one may and must deceive the old lady, for she is very stupid — evidently they have frightened her with my name. Do not give my name, but present my poems to her under the name of anybody you please . . . she is awfully dull-witted, but nevertheless tractable enough. The main thing is for my name not to get to her, and then everything will be smooth enough."

20

"To the sea" (autograph manuscript)

"*Moriu*" (1824)

Kilgour 1337

Ever since Byron's death at Missolonghi on 19 April 1824, Viazemsky had been harping at Pushkin to write something glorifying his memory. Finally on 24–25 June 1824, Pushkin wrote him: "you are sad about Byron, but I am very glad of his death as a sublime subject for poetry. As Byron's youth faded, so did his genius. In his tragedies, not excepting even *Cain*, he is no longer that fiery demon who created the Giaour and Childe Harold. The first two cantos of *Don Juan* are superior to the following ones. His poetry underwent a noticeable change. He was created completely back to front; there was no gradualness in him, he suddenly matured and grew up, sang his song and fell silent . . . . I promise you, however, some scribblings on His Excellency's death." True to his word, the valedictory ode "To the Sea" (given as "*K moriu*" in modern editions), occasioned by his enforced departure from Odessa in August 1824 for his mother's countryseat, Mikhailovskoe, in the province of Pskov, contains the following passage (ll. 40–50). It is one of the very rare reminiscences of Byron in Pushkin's lyrics:

And following him [Napoleon], like the noise of the storm,
Another genius fled away from us,
Another ruler of our thoughts.

He vanished, lamented by freedom,
Leaving his garland to the world.
Resound, be enraged by foul weather:
He was, o sea, your bard.

Your image was stamped on him,
He was created by your spirit:
Like you, powerful, deep, and gloomy,
Like you, by nothing tamed.

Могучей страстью очарован
У берегов остался я.

О чем жалеть? куда бы ныне
Я путь беспечный устремил?
Один предмет в твоей пустыне
Мою бы душу поразил.

Одна скала, гробница славы.
Там погружались в хладный сон
Воспоминанья величавы...
Там угасал Наполеон.

Там он почил среди мучений —
И вслед за ним, как бури шум,
Другой от нас умчался гений,
Другой властитель наших дум...

Взволнуйся, море, непогодой
Твой, [illegible], твой певец
Исчез, оплаканный свободой,
Оставя миру [illegible]

Мир опустел... ? Куда же
Ты вынес, океан?
Судьба земли повсюду та же
Где капля блага, там на страже
Уж просвещенье иль тиран

Прощай же, море, не забуду
Твоей торжественной красы
И долго, долго слышать буду
Твой гул в вечерний час

В леса в пустыни молчаливы
Перенесу тобою полн
Твои скалы, твои заливы
И блеск и тень и говор волн

Исчез оплаканный свободой
Оставя миру свой венец

Твой образ был на нем означен
Он духом создан был твоим
Как ты, глубок, могущ и мрачен
Как ты ничем неукротим

In the holograph manuscript of the poem, written on both sides of a folio leaf, with many cancellations and additions, lines 43–50 read:

Be enraged, [o] sea, by foul weather
Howl, [your] beloved son, your bard
Has vanished, lamented by freedom,
Leaving his garland to the world.

Your image was stamped on him—
He was created by your Spirit
He was, like you, deep and gloomy
Like you, by nothing tamed.

The passage gave Pushkin many difficulties and the final version we know is not reflected entirely in the autograph. The text of the Houghton Library manuscript is close but not identical with the poem's first publication in the almanac *Mnemosyne*, IV, 1824 (issued in October 1825).

The manuscript, acquired from the Diaghilev estate, was published in facsimile by Dmitry Čiževsky in the *Harvard Library Bulletin*, VIII (1954), and fully described and annotated in *Russian Literary Archives*, ed. Dmitry Čiževsky and Michael Karpovich (New York, 1956), pp. 5–39.

21

Vladimir Vasil'evich Izmailov (1773–1830), *editor*, The Literary museum for 1827.

Literaturnyi muzeum na 1827 god, ili, Vladimira Izmailova. **Moscow, 1827.**

Kilgour 640

On 9 October 1826, Pushkin wrote V. V. Izmailov, editor since 1814 of *The Messenger of Europe*: "I rejoice that I may in some way oblige the first estimable sponsor of my muse. Without fail I will convey to Vasilii L'vovich [Pushkin's uncle] some poems for your almanac." Pushkin's "*Solovei*" ("The Nightingale," later renamed "*Solovei i roza*") and "*Ispanskaia pesnia*" ("Spanish Song," later renamed "*Nochnoi zefir*") appeared with first publications by his uncle, Zhukovsky, Gnedich, Glinka, Viazemsky, etc.

22

Boris Mikhailovich Fedorov (1798–1875), *editor*, Memorial of the fatherland's muses.

Pamiatnik otechestvennykh muz. **St. Petersburg, 1827.**

Kilgour 813

The first appearance of six of Pushkin's poems in this almanac, divided into separately numbered prose and verse sections, aptly reveals the literary "ethics" of the period and the extent of an author's rights. Pushkin regarded B. M. Fedorov as an unprincipled literary hack and ridiculed the works and criticism of this "Northern bumblebee": "It is time for intelligence and knowledge to supplant Bulgarin and Fedorov" (letter to Pogodin, 1 July 1828.) Fedorov published the poems, five of which were lyrics written by Pushkin at the Lycée, without any knowledge, much less the permission of their author. He was brazen enough to write in his editor's preface: "Those who revere the modesty that adorns resplendent genius will be pleased to learn that Aleksandr Sergeevich Pushkin, having permitted the editor to include several of the first works of his Muse in this Almanac, and not trusting their merit, wished the editor to indicate the date of their composition. But the mature gift of genius is evident in these works of the young Poet, and for that they are even more precious for the *Memorial of the Fatherland's Muses.*" Pushkin had no recourse but to the pages of another publication, his friend Del'vig's *Northern Flowers for 1829*, which stated: "*In Memorial of the Muses*, fragments of Pushkin's poem 'The Faun and the Shepherdess,' a poem which the poet himself now repudiates, were published, and he has charged us with attesting this to the reading public." Fedorov continued his thievery unabashed in the second issue (also in the Kilgour collection), with the sub-title "An almanac for the lovers of literature" (St. Petersburg, 1828). No more volumes were published.

23

The Northern lyre for 1827.

Severnaia lira na 1827 god.
Moscow, 1827.

Diaghilev-Lifar library 26

This almanac was edited by D. P. Oznobishin (1804–77), a poet and translator of Arabian literature, and S. E. Raich (1792–1855), poet and translator, most remembered now as the mentor of Fedor Tiutchev and as the inspirer of the Moscow "Society of Friends," which championed the "new" German metaphysics and Romantic literature. It is open to a sonnet by Vasilii Ivanovich Tumansky (1800–60) "On the Death of R," dated "Odessa, July 1825" and inscribed to Pushkin. Tumansky, a minor poet and Pushkin's fellow clerk in Count Mikhail Vorontsov's Odessa Chancery, certainly knew of Pushkin's jealous passion for the "R" of this sonnet, Amalia Riznich, the wife of a Dalmatian merchant. Pushkin courted her with success in the summer and autumn of 1823, and addressed to her, scholars believe, the magnificent elegy "My voice for you, caressing, langorous." In 1826, when Pushkin learned of her death in Genoa in May 1825, he wrote "Beneath the blue sky of her native land" to her memory, and in 1830 the even more famous "For the shores of your distant country." Pushkin's draft review of the volume, of course, makes no mention of Tumansky's sonnet, although it remarks that his other works in the almanac "reveal a decided talent." Pushkin takes no note of the contributions of the young Fedor Tiutchev (1803–73), among them translations of Goethe, Schiller, Byron, and the first published Russian translation of Heine (his "*Ein Fichtenbaum steht einsam,*" entitled "*S chuzhoi storony*"). The censor for the almanac was Aleksei Merzliakov (1778–1830), poet, literary theorist, and professor of literature at Moscow University. He had encouraged the fledgling poetic efforts of Tiutchev, and first read one of his works in public, to a gathering of the Moscow Society of the Amateurs of Russian Literature in 1818.

The Northern lyre for 1827, recognized by contemporaries as one of the best of its time, was reprinted with commentaries in the Soviet Union in 1984.

24

The Polar star . . . for 1827.

Poliarnaia zvezda . . . na 1825 god.
St. Petersburg, 1825.

Diaghilev-Lifar library 22

Aleksandr Bestuzhev had made an annual survey of Russian literature a fixture of the serious almanacs since the 1823 issue of *Polar Star.* Pushkin admired the practice, if not always Bestuzhev's views. He upbraided him for the careless way he and Ryleev had published his poems in the number for 1824, but he made no comment on Bestuzhev's survey, in which he traced the complete "inanition" of Russian literature to the "latent passion for Gallicisms" that had afflicted everyone since the end of the War of 1812–14. Pushkin, of course, realized that his own works could be accused of this, but he merely joked about linguistic habits in a letter to Viazemsky: "I hate to see in our primevally wild language any traces of European affectation and French refinement. Coarseness and simplicity suit it better. I preach from internal conviction, but as is my custom, I write otherwise (between 1 and 8 December 1823).

Pushkin took strong exception, however, to the "Glance at Russian Literature in the Course of 1824 and at the Beginning of 1825," to which the volume on display is open. It provoked the draft of a long reply (published only in 1934) and a letter to its author (end of May/beginning of June 1825), two of Pushkin's most important statements on the condition of Russian letters of the day. He challenged Bestuzhev's periodization of literary history and his contention that the "first period" of every literature had "always been an age of strong emotions and works of genius." Using Latin, Italian, English, and especially Russian literature as examples, Pushkin disputed Bestuzhev point by point, concluding in his letter, "Your words are fully applicable to French literature alone."

Bestuzhev's remark "We have criticism, but we have no literature" particularly irritated Pushkin. In his draft article he asked: "We have criticism? Where then is it? Where are our Addisons, La Harpes, Schlegels, Sismondis? What have we analyzed critically? Whose literary opinions have been accepted as typical of

Russian culture? Whose critical works can we use for reference and support?" "Just where did you get that idea?," he wrote to Bestuzhev: "Criticism is just what we lack. . . . We have not a single commentary, not a single book of criticism . . . Just what are you calling criticism? *The Messenger of Europe* and *The Well-Intentioned*?. . . . This cannot establish any kind of real opinion among our public, it cannot be dignified as a code of taste. . . . No, let us say your phrase the other way around: We have literature of a sort, but we have no criticism. . . . With only one people did criticism precede literature—with the Germans."

25

ASP, Poems of Aleksandr Pushkin.

Stikhotvoreniia Aleksandra Pushkina.
St. Petersburg, 1826.

Kilgour 878

Pushkin had been trying to bring out a volume of his collected verse since 1820. Prince Aleksandr Lobanov-Rostovsky broached the idea in 1822 and Viazemsky raised it in 1824, but Pushkin wrote him that the proposal was "unrealizable, and here's why: in 1820 I copied out my rubbish and intended to publish it by subscription; I printed tickets and disposed of about forty. Then I lost my manuscript [at cards] to Nikita Vsevolozhky (of course, with a certain proviso). Meanwhile I have been compelled to flee from Mecca to Medina, my Koran started going from hand to hand, and true believers are still awaiting it. Now I have given my brother the task of seeking out and buying back my manuscript, and then we shall proceed to the publication of the elegies, epistles, and the miscellaneous things" (29 November 1824).

Pushkin's brother Lev finally succeeded in recovering the manuscript from Vsevolozhsky (1799–1862) in the spring of 1825. Pushkin immediately gave the collection a thorough revision, correcting earlier texts and amending poems written after 1820. By the summer he gave up on using his bumbling and not altogether honest brother as his literary agent ("such another shameless agent as Lev does not exist and never will"—letter to Del'vig, 1–8 June 1825). He gave Petr Aleksandrovich Pletnev (1792–1865), a scrupulous man of letters, the assignment of seeing the book into print. The volume, divided into "Elegies, Various Poems, Epigrams and Inscriptions, Imitations of the Ancients, Epistles, and Imitations of the Koran," appeared on 28 December 1825. "The edition is very nice; there are mistakes here and there, but nothing to speak of" (letter to Pletnev, January 1826). Karamzin, to whom Pletnev presented the volume, was horrified by the epigraph —"*aetas prima canat veneres, extrema tumultus*"—from the *Elegies* (Bk. II, No. X, l. 7) of Sextus Propertius. He understood *tumultus* as a veiled allusion to the Decembrist insurrection. Pletnev explained that the book had been printed long before that event of 14 December 1825, and that anyway Pushkin meant "the soul's tumult."

The Kilgour collection also contains the first edition of *Poems* (St. Petersburg, 1829), Parts 1 and 2, organized chronologically; the similarly arranged third part (1832); and the fourth part (1835), divided into "Fairy Tales" (*skazki*) and "Songs of the Western Slavs." The four parts are bound together into two volumes. The two-volume *Poemy i povesti* (*Narrative Poems and Tales*) of 1835 is also in the collection.

NARRATIVE POEMS

The items in this case, Pushkin's narrative poems from the 1820's, chart the trajectory of his rising and falling popularity with the reading public (such as it was) and of his hopes for a literary profession (or "trade" as he ironically called it). From the modest success of *Ruslan and Liudmila*, to the unexpected and unprecedented triumph of *The Fountain of Bakhchisarai*, to the no less surprising failure of *Poltava*, the story of their publication and reception reveals many of the pitfalls that awaited an aspiring writer of the time. This is especially true if we extend the trajectory to include Pushkin's greatest narrative poem, *The Bronze Horseman* (1833), which he could not, for reasons of censorship, print during his lifetime. As impressive, indeed mind-boggling, as his honorarium for *The Fountain of Bakhchisarai* proved to be, it must be noted that these 3,000 rubles, while they would have supported a low-ranking government clerk for several years, would not have covered the cost of one of his future wife's ball gowns.

The narrative poems also illustrate the development of Russian criticism during the decade, which began with literature still in the hands of salon amateurs, nameless scribes, teachers and students and which witnessed the rise of the first Russian "bestsellers" in verse and prose fiction. Pushkin's first poems were often reviewed with what he called "proofreaders" comments, i.e. minor quibbles about grammar, style, and lexicon that were more suitable for private discussion than for public criticism. But *Poltava* was issued and reviewed in the midst of a savage public controversy between Pushkin and Bulgarin, in which the latter sought by all available means, foul and more foul, to compromise Pushkin with the reading public. Neither type of criticism could hope to bridge the gap between readers and writers that arises when literature leaves the classroom or salon and enters the modern public sphere.

Meanwhile, Pushkin's narrative poems served as the focus for many debates about literary style, characterization, genre, and theme as well as about the moral and civic responsibility of literature. Beyond this, their poetics of fragmentation, of hints and ellipses, made them narratives for the imaginative reader. Viazemsky, who had been somewhat critical of the "unfinished" hero in *A Prisoner of the Caucasus*, endorsed this new poetics enthusiastically in a dialogue with which he prefaced the first edition of *The Fountain of Bakhchisarai*: "In a speech, frequent pronouns retard its flow and cool off its exposition. Invention and fantasy also have their *pronouns*, which talent tries to avoid with felicitous ellipses. Why express and emphasize everything, when we are dealing with people of active and keen understanding?"

W M T

26

ASP, Ruslan and Liudmila.
First edition.

Ruslan i Liudmila.
St. Petersburg, 1820.

Kilgour 874

"To the victorious pupil from the defeated teacher on that most solemn day when he finished his poem *Ruslan and Liudmila*, Mar. 26, 1820, Good Friday." So Zhukovsky wrote when he presented his portrait, a lithograph by E. Oesterreich, in recognition of his young friend's achievement. The apostrophe to "the friends of *Ruslan and Liudmila*" in *Eugene Onegin* (One, II, 5) reflects the general acclaim which greeted the work's publication in June 1820. By then the author was far from the capital, in southern Russia, and he had to wait almost a year before actually seeing a copy of his mock epic in six cantos, on which he had worked since 1817.

Mikhail Glinka instinctively realized the West European inspiration of this spirited fairy tale, thoroughly epicurean in its vibrant and lightly ironic tone, when he utilized it for his delightful Italianate opera of the same title (1842). Russian

folklore had never sounded so good, but then it provided window dressing only to this "first Russian masterpiece in the narrative genre" (Nabokov). Pushkin himself later cast a sober eye on his first public success, in the uncompleted "Refutation of Criticism" (1830): "*Ruslan and Liudmila* was on the whole favorably received. . . . Nobody even noticed that it is a cold work. It was charged with being immoral because of a few somewhat voluptuous descriptions, some lines which I excluded from the second edition . . . and the parody of [Zhukovsky's] 'The Twelve Sleeping Maidens.' I could have been soundly taken to task for the last of these, for showing a lack of esthetic sensibility. It was unforgiveable (particularly at my age) to parody a maidenly poetic creation for the pleasure of the mob. The other criticisms were rather shallow. Is there even one place in *Ruslan* which could be compared in the license of its jokes to the pranks of, for example, even Ariosto, of whom I was constantly being reminded? Why even the part I omitted was a very toned-down imitation of Ariosto (*Orlando*, Canto V, st. viii)."

The Kilgour copy is open to the frontispiece, drawn by Ivan Ivanov from a sketch by Aleksei Olenin, depicting four scenes from the poem. It delighted Pushkin, who wrote to Gnedich (who had seen the manuscript through the press): "The clothing tailored by your order for *Ruslan and Liudmila* is beautiful; for some four whole days the printed verse, the vignettes, and the binding have been giving me childish pleasure. I cordially thank the esteemed Ꭿ; these strokes of the pen are sweet proof to me of his amiable good will" (24 March 1821).

27

ASP, Ruslan and Liudmila. Second edition.

Ruslan i Liudmila.
St. Petersburg, 1828.

Kilgour 874.1

Pushkin was determined not to repeat the financial experience of the first edition of *Ruslan and Liudmila*, which, despite its public success, had brought him virtually nothing. The bookseller I. V. Slenin had bought up the copies and then made Pushkin infrequent payments, usually sending books instead of badly needed cash. At Pushkin's request, Viazemsky agreed in 1823 to see to a second edition. Pushkin dropped some "offending passages" to satisfy the censor, and added the famous prologue, written 1825–26. This revised, enlarged edition did not, however, appear until 1828. Pushkin also included a witty preface (dated 12 February 1828). The volume is open to the engraving by N. I. Utkin (1780–1863) after Orest Kiprensky's portrait of the poet. Del'vig had commissioned the work from Kiprensky in 1827; Pushkin used 1,000 rubles from the purchase price for *Boris Godunov* to buy it from Del'vig's widow in 1831.

28

ASP, A prisoner of the Caucasus.

Kavkazskii plennik : povest'.
St. Petersburg, 1822.

Kilgour 875

This first of Pushkin's so-called "Southern Poems," begun in August 1820, finished in the spring of 1821, and published in the last week of August 1822, delighted the reading public far more than it did the author himself, who was no sooner done with it than he was belittling its accomplishment in letters to friends. "It is evident from your letter that you expected a great deal—you will find little, very little" (to Gnedich, 24 March 1821); "Altogether I am very displeased with my poem, and consider it much inferior to *Ruslan*, although its verses are more mature" (to V. P. Gorchakov, October-November 1822). He hoped to make a nice profit from its publication, but made the mistake of allowing Gnedich to see it into print. Gnedich made 5,000 rubles for his efforts, sending the author 500 and a free copy. Pushkin graciously thanked him in a letter, but did not use Gnedich as an agent again.

In the 1830 "Refutation of Criticism," he wrote: "A *Prisoner of the Caucasus*—my first unsuccessful attempt at characterization, with which I coped with difficulty. It was received better than anything else I had written, thanks to certain elegiac and descriptive verses. But on the other hand Nikolai [to whom the poem is dedicated] and Aleksandr Raevsky and I had a good laugh at it."

The volume is open to Egor Geitman's (1800–29) engraving of the young Pushkin, which was accompanied by this note: "The publishers add a portrait of the Author, drawn in his youth. They believe it is pleasant to preserve the young features of a Poet whose first works are marked by an unusual gift." Pushkin (in a letter to Gnedich) wondered if it resembled him very much, but considered the note "extremely flattering." The Kilgour collection also contains the second corrected edition of 1828, as well as the edition of 1824 in which a German translation (*Der Berggefangene*) by A. E. Wulffert (unnamed here) faces the Russian text.

No.27:
ASP (from no. 58)

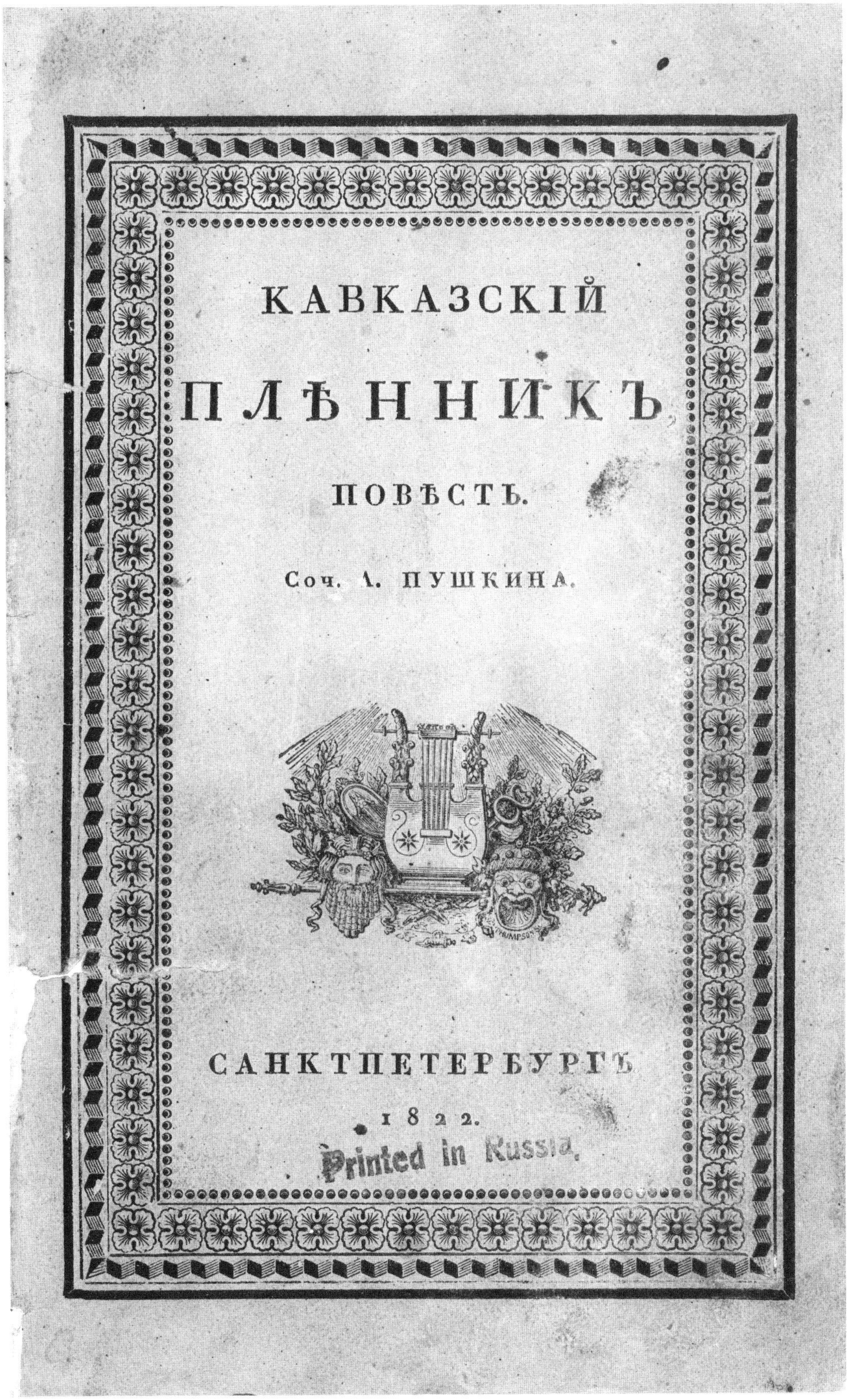

КАВКАЗСКІЙ

ПЛѢННИКЪ

ПОВѢСТЬ.

Соч. А. ПУШКИНА.

САНКТПЕТЕРБУРГЪ

1822.

No.28

29

ASP, The fountain of Bakhchisarai.

Bakhchisaraiskii fontan.
Moscow, 1824.

Kilgour 876

This Oriental romance, written at Kishinev in the first part of 1822 and published 10 March 1824, was the first Russian "bestseller" in verse (Pushkin received 3,000 rubles; "Incidentally, I wrote it solely for myself, but I am publishing it because I need the money" [to Bestuzhev, 8 February 1824.]) On 14 October 1823 Pushkin confessed to Viazemsky: "Between ourselves, the Fountain of Bakhchisarai is trash, but its epigraph is delightful." Later, too, Pushkin (in "Refutation of Criticism") wrote that he considered the prose motto, adapted from the Persian poet Sadi (as quoted in Moore's *Lalla Rookh*)—"Many, like me, have visited this Fountain; but some are no more, others are journeying far"—"better than the whole poem," and he echoed its second half in the final stanza of *Eugene Onegin* (Eight, LI, 3–4).

The "Refutation of Criticism" contains a hard-headed appraisal of this example of Pushkin's Byronic Orientalia: "*The Fountain of Bakhchisarai* is weaker than *A Prisoner* and, like it, recalls my reading of Byron, over whom I had gone mad. The scene between Zarema and Maria [the two harem protagonists and rivals] has dramatic merit. It wasn't, it seems, criticized. . . . Young writers in general are unable to describe the physical movements of the passions. Their heroes always shudder, laugh wildly, gnash their teeth, etc. All this is ludicrous, like a melodrama."

Viazemsky, to whom Pushkin entrusted the printing of the manuscript, prefaced the first edition with his own "A Conversation between the Publisher and A Classicist from the Vyborg Side or from Vasil'evsky Island," one of the most important and brilliant critical manifestoes of what was called Romanticism in Russia at the time.

The Kilgour collection also contains Alexander Wulffert's German translation, *Der Trauerquell* (St. Petersburg, 1826), with four original engravings by Galaktionov and a fold-out "Tataren-Lied" by L. Maurer at the end; the second edition of 1827, with the same engraved plate illustrations of Galaktionov; the third edition of 1830; and William D. Lewis's first translation into English of *The Bakchesarian Fountain by Alexander Pooshkeen, and Other Poems by Various Authors* (Philadelphia, 1849).

30

ASP, The bandit brothers : written in 1822.

Brat'ia razboiniki : pisano v 1822 godu.
Moscow, 1827.

Kilgour 881

Pushkin was so dissatisfied with this lurid verse tale, written in 1821–22 and conceived as a long narrative poem, that he burnt most of it ("it served them right," letter to Bestuzhev of 13 June 1823). A fragment that survived the *auto-da-fé* appeared in the *Polar Star for 1825* and then as this separate edition (the second edition of the same year is also in the Kilgour collection). In a letter to Viazemsky of 11 November 1823, Pushkin wrote that the work was based on a "true occurrence": "In 1820, during my stay in Ekaterinoslavl, two bandits, chained together, swam across the Dnepr and escaped. Their resting on the little island and the drowning of one of the guards are not my invention. Certain verses remind one of the translation of *The Prisoner of Chillon* [1822]. That is my misfortune. I coincided with Zhukovsky by accident, my fragment was written at the end of 1821."

31

ASP, The gypsies : written in 1824.

Tsygany : pisano v 1824 godu.
Moscow, 1827.

Kilgour 880

This romantic poem, begun in the winter of 1823 in Odessa and finished on 10 October 1824, at Mikhailovskoe, is generally considered the finest of the "Southern Poems," and it has inspired the most diverse, often controversial, critical reaction since its anonymous publication in May 1827. Long before then, the work, reflecting Pushkin's stay in Bessarabia, was well-known in literary circles because of Lev Pushkin's habit of reciting his brother's verse in public and passing about manu-

(359)

БРАТЬЯ РАЗБОЙНИКИ.

(Отрывокъ изъ Поэмы.)

Не стая вороновъ слеталась
На груды тлѣющихъ костей,
За Волгой, ночью, вкругъ огней
Удалыхъ шайка собиралась.
Какая смѣсь одеждъ и лицъ,
Племенъ, нарѣчій, состояній:
Изъ хатъ, изъ келій, изъ темницъ
Они стеклися для стяжаній!
Здѣсь цѣль одна для всѣхъ сердецъ —
Живутъ безъ власти, безъ закона.
Межъ ними зрится и бѣглецъ
Съ бреговъ воинственнаго Дона,
И въ черныхъ локонахъ Еврей,
И дикіе сыны степей —
Калмыкъ, Башкирецъ безобразной,
И рыжій Финнъ, и съ лѣнью праздной
Вездѣ кочующій Цыганъ!
Опасность, кровь, развратъ, обманъ —
Вотъ узы страшнаго семейства;
Тотъ ихъ, кто съ каменной душой
Прошелъ всѣ ужасы злодѣйства;
Кто грабитъ хладною рукой
Вдовицу съ бѣдной сиротой,

No.30:
illustration by Galaktionov for *The bandit brothers* (from no. 24)

script copies. Pushkin repeatedly asked his brother to refrain from this; his fear of piece-by-piece pilfering of a new work necessitated publication before the poet felt ready. To Pushkin's great irritation, Lev ignored his admonitions with *The Gypsies.* He recited it to Bestuzhev, who mentioned it in his "glance" at Russian literature in the *Polar Star for 1825.* Zhukovsky, too, heard it and wrote Pushkin about it, to which he replied late in April 1825: "You ask what is the aim of *The Gypsies*? Here it is! The aim of poetry is poetry, as Del'vig says (if he didn't steal it)."

In "Refutation of Criticism" he ironically replied to those who had accused him of debunking the Romantic hero: "One lady remarked *à propos* of *The Gypsies* that in the whole poem there is only one honest person, and that is the bear. The late Ryleev indignantly asked why Aleko [the protagonist] leads the bear about and even collects money from the gaping crowd. Viazemsky also repeated the reproof. (Ryleev asked me to make Aleko at least a smith, which would be far more fitting.) The best thing would have been to have made him a civil servant of the eighth rank or a landowner, but not a gypsy. In that case, it is true, the whole poem would not have existed, *ma tanto meglio.*"

32

ASP, Count Nulin.

Graf Nulin.
St. Petersburg, 1827.

Kilgour 879

"At the end of 1825 I was living in the country. Rereading *Lucrece*, a rather weak poem of Shakespeare's, I thought: what if it had occurred to Lucrece to slap Tarquin's face? Perhaps this would have cooled off his enterprise, and he would have been obliged to withdraw, covered with shame. Lucrece would not have stabbed herself, Publicola would not have been enraged, Brutus would not have driven out the kings, and the world and the history of the world would have been different.

And so we owe the republic, the consuls, the dictators, the Catos, the Caesars, to a seduction similar to one which took place recently in my neighborhood, in the Novorzhev district.

I was struck by the idea of parodying history and Shakespeare. I could not resist the double temptation, and in two mornings had written this tale.

I am accustomed to date my papers. *Count Nulin* was written on December 13 and 14 [the date of the Decembrist uprising]. Strange coincidences do occur."—"A Note on *Count Nulin*," 1830.

The poem was first published in the almanac, *Northern Flowers for 1828*.

33

ASP, Poltava : poema.

St. Petersburg, 1829.

Kilgour 883

Pushkin had long been fascinated by the figure of Peter the Great, and his "dialogue" with Peter and his legacy, which intensified in the 1830's in a series of historical investigations and literary works, first found major expression in this romantic historical epic written in the course of 1828 and celebrating Peter's triumph over Charles XII of Sweden. Pushkin feared that the abrupt Shifts from romance (the story of Maria Kochubei and her godfather, the Hetman Mazeppa, who betrays Peter) to national epic (Peter's struggles with Charles) in the narrative, which culminates in an exultant description of the battle of Poltava, would baffle critics and readers alike. The work, with an epigraph from Byron's *Mazeppa*—"The power and glory of the war / Faithless os [sic] their vain votaries, men, / Had pass'd to the triumphant Czar"—was a dismal commercial and critical failure.

Pushkin responded point by point in "Refutation of Criticism," but had to admit "defeat" ("How can one answer such criticisms?"): "*Habent sua fata libelli*. *Poltava* had no success. Probably it did not deserve any, but I had been spoiled by the reception given my previous, far weaker works. Furthermore it is a completely original work, which is what we are struggling for." Two years later he wrote to Mikhail Pogodin (1800–75): "I'm told that you have been given a sharp scolding for [*Marfa the Novgorod*] *Burgomaster's Wife*: I hope this will have no influence whatever on your labors. Remember that for ten years in a row they praised me for God knows what, but they really criticized me for *Godunov* and *Poltava*. With us criticism is of course beneath not only literature itself, but even the public. One may become angry with it, but to put any credence whatever in it is unforgiveable weakness" (11 July 1832).

The volume is open to Pushkin's inscription "To His High Excellency Gracious Sir Ivan Ivanovich Dmitriev from the Author." Pushkin had known and criticized Dmitriev for years, but retained a certain fondness for him as one of his literary "grandfathers."

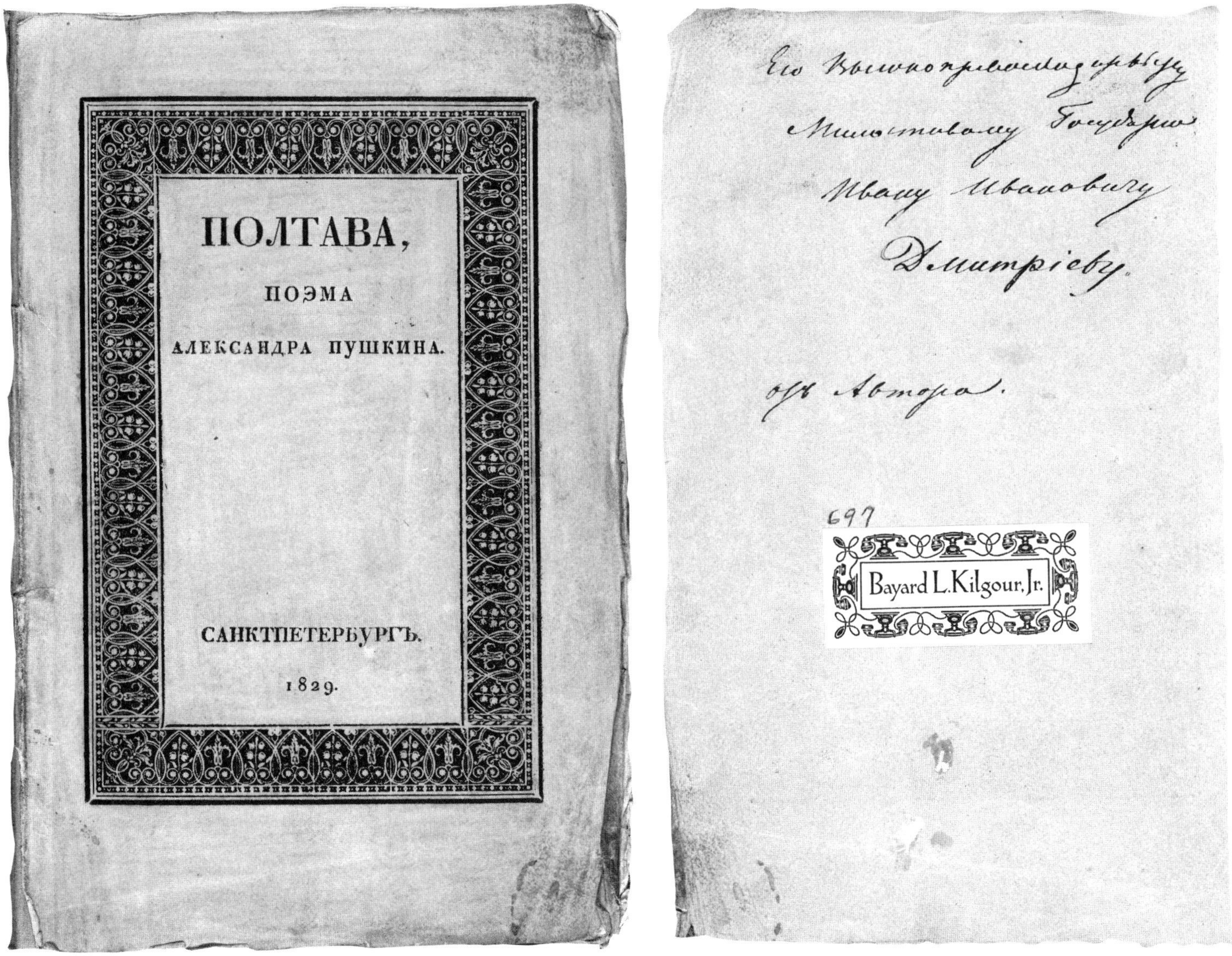

No. 33:
front wrapper, with inscription on verso by ASP

·V·

EUGENE ONEGIN

Vissarion Belinsky (1811–48) hailed Pushkin's "novel in verse" as "an encyclopedia of Russian life" and a realist masterpiece. A later age prefers to see it as an encyclopedia of literature itself, nineteenth-century Russia's meta-literary classic *par excellence*, or, more recently, as an exemplary illustration of Zhukovsky's apt characterization of society: "a vast theater where each is at once actor and spectator."

Pushkin began his "free novel" in Kishinev on 9 May 1823 (the third anniversary of his expulsion from St. Petersburg), and brought it to completion more than eight years later, on 5 October 1831 in Tsarskoe Selo. His preoccupation with it "lasted longer (1822–35) than the span of life actually devoted to its composition," as Nabokov noted. As late as September 1835, he toyed with the idea of again refracting the characters in the "magic crystal" of his imagination. The "openness" of the novel's ending prompted several unsuccessful attempts in the nineteenth century to take further the story of Eugene and Tatiana, the two main protagonists, who lived on throughout the century as prototypes for scores of other literary heroes and heroines and as the inspiration for Tchaikovsky's "modest work" of 1878. "I should like to call it 'lyrical scenes,' or something of that kind. This opera has no future!" (letter to Sergei Taneev, 2 January 1878).

Viazemsky was the first of Pushkin's friends to learn of the work when the poet wrote him on 4 November 1823: "As to my occupations, I am now writing not a novel, but a novel in verse—a devil of a difference. It's in the genre of Don Juan. Publication is unthinkable; I'm writing the way I feel like it. Our censorship is so whimsical that it is impossible to shape a course of action—better not to think about it at all." Twelve days later he wrote to his old schoolmate Del'vig: "I am now writing a new narrative poem in which I chatter beyond all limits. Birukov [the censor] shall not see it because he is a fie-baby, a capricious child." And on 1 December, the title first appeared in the poet's correspondence, when he wrote his lifelong friend and stanch supporter Aleksandr Turgenev: "In my leisure hours I am now writing a new narrative poem, *Eugene Onegin*, wherein I choke on my bile. Two cantos are already ready."

Pushkin worried about the fate of his work with the censorship throughout 1824, by which time fragments were already being read and recited in salons and literary circles. The publisher Slenin offered "as much as I want for *Onegin*" in the spring; "So there's Russia for you, why she really is in Europe, and I thought it was a mistake of the geographers," as Pushkin went on in his letter to Viazemsky (early April 1824). By then, unbeknownst to Pushkin, Faddei Bulgarin had already pirated ten lines from the first chapter, and by the end of the year, Del'vig, with Pushkin's sanction, published parts of Chapter Two in his genteel *Northern Flowers*. On 28 December 1824, the censor passed Chapter One and the formal publishing history of "life's novel" began.

34

Faddei Venediktovich Bulgarin (1789–1859), *editor*, Literary leaflets.

***Literaturnye listki*. Pt. 1, no. IV. St. Petersburg, 1824.**

The February 1824 issue of Bulgarin's slightly disreputable "journal of manners and literature" is open to its "Literary News," where a passage from *Eugene Onegin* (One, XX, 5-14) first appeared in print (the number also contains two of Pushkin's lyrics). "One enlightened admirer of Literature," the editor commented,

> has written us from Kiev that the narrative poem *Onegin* is the finest work of the inimitable Pushkin. We beg the esteemed Author's pardon for daring to publish without his knowledge several lines from *Onegin* that were brought here in someone's head and dictated from memory, and therefore may contain errors (not noticed by us at any rate). This is the description of Russia's prima ballerina:
>
> Then with a half-ethereal splendour,
> bound where the magic bow will send her,
> Istómina, thronged all around
> by Naiads, one foot on the ground,
> twirls the other slowly as she pleases,
> then suddenly she's off, and there

ЛИТЕРАТУРНЫЕ ЛИСТКИ.

1824.

№ 5.

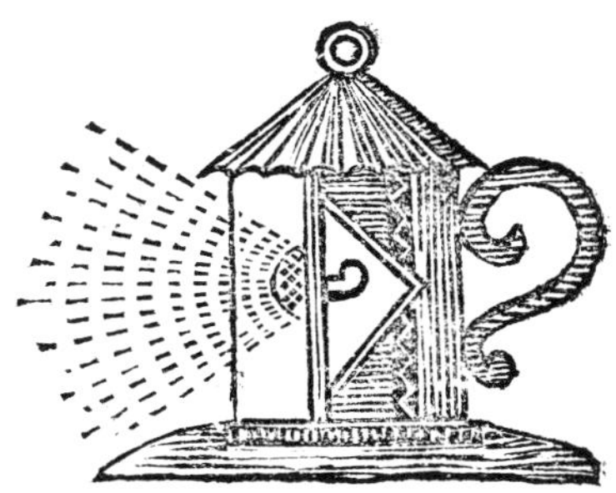

she's up and flying through the air
like fluff before Aeolian breezes;
she'll spin this way and that, and beat
against each other swift, small feet.
[Charles Johnston tr.]

What a living picture! What true Poetry! . . . In our opinion, not a single Russian Poet possesses Pushkin's magic power for fixing ephemeral objects with a glance (*fixer les objets*) and for making living pictures from them. His imagination is a mirror in which nature is reflected in its true aspect: Poetry has entrusted him with her colors, and the Genius of Elegance his brush. But until now the Charites alone have governed his ardent soul. There will come a time, however, when consequential Muses will draw the attention of their young charge, and will show him subjects in the affairs of our Fatherland worthy of his sublime talent.

Bulgarin compounded his theft by republishing the lines in his theatrical review *The Russian Thalia* (also in the Kilgour collection) in mid-December of the same year. The issue also contained a portrait engraving of Evdokiia Istomina (1799–1848), the ballerina who had danced the Cherkessian girl in Didelot's ballet derived from *A Prisoner of the Caucasus* in 1823.

When Bulgarin could no longer steal from Pushkin with impunity, and when *The Literary Gazette* threatened to offer a serious commercial challenge to his four-sheet rag, the *Northern Bee*, he became the poet's most bitter and unscrupulous literary enemy.

35

Baron Anton Antonovich Del'vig (1798-1831), *editor*, Northern flowers [for 1825].

Severnye tsvety.
St. Petersburg, 1825.

Kilgour 1049

Out of his old friendship for its editor, Del'vig, Pushkin donated to his new almanac a fragment from the Second Chapter of *Eugene Onegin* (VII,1–8, VIII,1–9, IX–X,1–12), the first (excluding Bulgarin's pirated one) to appear in print. The publication of the issue was held up by the terrible flood of 7 November 1824 ("I am sorry about Del'vig's *Flowers*; and will this delay him long in the Petersburg mire?"—early 20's of November 1824, to his brother), later the subject of *The Bronze Horseman*. Three of Pushkin's lyrics ("The Song of Oleg the Seer," "The Demon," "Proserpine"), as well as verse by Krylov, Zhukovsky, Baratynsky, Viazemsky, Glinka, and Del'vig himself also graced the elegant volume, which is open to "Passages from *Eugene Onegin*, a Long Poem by A. Pushkin."

The Kilgour collection contains all eight volumes of the famous almanac, in which other fragments of *Onegin* appeared in the issues for 1826, 1827 (Tatiana's letter), and 1830.

36

ASP, Eugene Onegin : a novel in verse.

***Evgenii Onegin : roman v stikhakh.* 7 v.**
St. Petersburg and Moscow, 1825–32.

Kilgour 877

Early in April 1824, writing to Viazemsky, Pushkin complained that the censorship problem facing Chapter One of *Onegin* "was no joking matter, for it is a question of my future fate, of the independence I need." Always short of money (his penny-pinching father disliked his eldest son intensely) and frequently in serious debt, the poet was not joking when he wrote to Viazemsky: "Since I do not belong to our writers of the eighteenth century [who enjoyed Imperial patronage], I write for myself, but I publish for money, and not in the slightest for a smile from the fair sex" (8 March 1824). When the journalist and critic Nikolai Nadezhdin (1804–56) criticized him for having published *Onegin* chapter by chapter, Pushkin defended himself with some heat in a letter to Mikhail Pogodin: "By the way, tell Nadezhdin that the recklessness of his judgments is unforgivable. Not long ago I

No.35:
Del'vig, from *Tsarskoe selo* (1830)

read in his journal [*The Telescope*, 1832, No. 9] a comparison between me and [the journalist-historian Nikolai] Polevoi; 'Both hoax the public: one swindles money from it by publishing his *Onegin* a chapter at a time, and the other his *History* a volume at a time.' The difference is between *collecting subscriptions, having promised* to publish twelve volumes in a year, and then in three years to publish three volumes on the interest from the swindled money—and of publishing, a chapter at a time, a work regarding which it is said in the preface: 'Here is the beginning of a poem which will probably never be finished.' Nadezhdin is at liberty to find my verses bad, but to compare me with a cheat is swinishness on his part" (11 July 1832).

***Chapter One* (SPb., 1825). First edition.**

The first edition of Chapter One, written in 1823, published on 16 February 1825, and dedicated to Lev Pushkin, who had seen to its publication, contained this brief Foreword (alluded to by Pushkin in his letter to Pogodin of 11 July 1832):

> Here is the beginning of a long poem which will probably not be finished.
>
> Several cantos or chapters of *Eugene Onegin* are already completed. Having been written under the influence of favorable circumstances, they bear the imprint of that gaiety which marked the first works of the author of *Ruslan and Liudmila.*
>
> The first chapter forms something complete in itself. It contains a description of the life of a young man in Petersburg society at the end of 1819 and is reminiscent of Beppo—a humorous work by the somber Byron.
>
> Far-sighted critics will, of course, note the want of a plan. Everyone is free to pass judgment on the plan of a whole novel on reading its first chapter. They will also deplore the anti-poetical nature of the main char-

acter, who tends somewhat to resemble the Prisoner of the Caucasus, as well as certain stanzas written in the depressing manner of the latest elegies "wherein the feeling of dejection engulfs all other feelings." But allow us to draw readers' attention to qualities rarely to be found in satirical writing: the absence of an abusive individual and the maintenance of strict decorum in the humorous description of manners.

The rhymed iambic tetrameter "A Conversation between a Bookseller and a Poet," completed 26 September 1824, followed. It appeared as a separate poem in the 1826 Poems. The Foreword was excluded from the 1833 complete edition.

The 1825 text also contains Pushkin's long note on his reference to "my Africa" (L,11) in this chapter: "The author, on his mother's side, is of African descent. His great-grandfather, Abram Petrovich Annibal, in his eighth year, was stolen from the shores of Africa and brought to Constantinople. The Russian envoy, having rescued him, sent him as a gift to Peter the Great . . . ." It concludes: "In Russia, where the memory of eminent men is soon obliterated owing to the absence of historical memoirs, the bizarre life of Annibal is known only through family tradition. We hope to publish his complete biography." Pushkin turned to the life of Annibal in his unfinished historical romance *The Blackamoor of Peter the Great* (*Arap Petra Velikogo*, 1827).

Aleksandr Bestuzhev and Ryleev, in terms reminiscent of Bulgarin's mild stricture in *Literary Leaflets*, both objected to the chapter's "lack of seriousness."

On 25 January 1825, Pushkin wrote Ryleev: "Bestuzhev writes me a lot about *Onegin*—tell him that he is wrong: does he really want to banish from the realm of poetry all that is light and gay? . . . This is rather strict. Pictures of society life also enter the realm of poetry." And on 24 March 1825, he wrote Bestuzhev: "Your letter is very clever, but all the same you are wrong, all the same you are looking at *Onegin* from the wrong point of view, all the same it is my best work. You compare the First Chapter with *Don Juan*. Nobody esteems *Don Juan* more than I do . . . but it has nothing in common with *Onegin*. . . . Where do I have satire? There is not a ghost of it in *Eugene Onegin*. . . . The very word *satirical* should not have occurred in my foreword. Wait till you see the other cantos. . . . Canto One is merely a rapid introduction, and I am pleased with it (which very seldom happens with me). Whereupon I conclude our polemic . . . ." The polemics had only begun.

Chapter Two (Moscow, 1826). First edition.

Chapter Two, written in less than two months at the end of 1823, appeared for sale on 20 October 1826. "On the paper wrapper is engraved a small stylized nymphalid butterfly, with half-closed wings and oversized abdomen, in profile" (Nabokov). The Kilgour collection also contains the second separate editions of Chapter One (1829) and Chapter Two (1830) bound in one volume.

Chapter Three (SPb., 1827). First edition.

Chapter Three, composed in the spring (at Odessa) and in the autumn (at Mikhailovskoe) of 1824, appeared almost exactly a year after the second, on 10 October 1827, with the following note: "The first chapter of *Eugene Onegin*, written in 1823, came out in 1825. Two years later, the second was published. This slowness proceeded from extrinsic circumstances. Henceforth publication will follow an uninterrupted order, one chapter coming immediately after another." The "extrinsic circumstances" involved Pushkin's having entrusted the printing of Chapter Two to his friend, the "sluggard" and "slob," Sergei Sobolevsky (1803–70), to whom he wrote in November 1827: "Stop writing stupidities to Anna [Kern], write me a sensible word. Where is the second part of *Onegin*? They're requesting it here [Petersburg] and on account of it the sale of other chapters has stopped. And who is to blame? You, Belly, Caliban, etc."

Chapters Four and Five (SPb., 1828). First edition.

After the fiasco with the printing of Chapter Two, Pushkin turned to the always reliable Petr Pletnev to see the remainder of the work into print. The grateful poet dedicated this first separate edition of Chapters Four and Five, published 31 January–2 February 1828, and later the whole work to him. On 27 May 1826, Pushkin confided to Viazemsky that in Chapter Four—begun in October 1824 and delayed from completion by work on *Boris Godunov* and *Count Nulin* until the first week of 1826—he had depicted his country life at Mikhailovskoe: "If the Tsar grants me my *freedom*, I won't stay [in Russia] another month. We live in a sorry era, but when I imagine London, railroads, steamships, the English journals or the theaters and bordellos of Paris—then my Mikhailovskoe backwoods make me sick and mad."

In the 1830 "Refutation of Criticism," Pushkin noted: "For a long time our critics left me in peace. This does them credit: my circumstances were far from favorable. Through habit they considered me still to be a very young man. The first hostile articles [in *The Atheneum* and *The Messenger of Europe*], as I remember, began to appear on the publication of the fourth and fifth cantos of *Eugene Onegin*." Pushkin was taken to task for portraying "immoral characters" and for various linguistic "liberties," which *The Atheneum* reviewer (M. A. Dmitriev) blamed on "Romanticism." It "rescues a poem from all pretensions to common sense and from the legitimate demands of taste." Pushkin set down a detailed reply to *The Atheneum*, but did not publish it, remarking: "Finally, he finds that these two chapters are good for nothing, about which I won't argue with him."

Chapter Six **(SPb., 1828). First edition.**

The first edition of this chapter, which seems to have been finished by December 1826 (the manuscript is lost), appeared 23 March 1828. It contained a long list of corrections of the "several serious mistakes" which had "crept into" the previous chapters. Pushkin at times liked to assume the pose of a dilettante "scribbler," but he took the publication of his works with the highest seriousness and was irritated by the misprints and manuscript misreadings which bedevilled them. "The sixth canto was not analyzed at all; in *The Messenger of Europe* they did not even note the Latin misprint [*sed altri tempora* instead of *sed alia tempora* in VII, 5] ("Refutation of Criticism").

Chapter Seven **(SPb., 1830). First edition.**

Work on this chapter—between July 1827 and November 1828—gave Pushkin more trouble than any of the others, and its publication on 18-19 March 1830 provoked a large number of unfavorable reviews. On 28 November 1830, at Boldino, he wrote out a preface for a planned, but never realized, separate edition of two chapters, "Eight" (now known as "Onegin's Journey") and "Nine" (the present Eight):

> With us, it is rather difficult for the author himself to learn the impression that his work produces upon the public. All he learns from the journals is their editors' opinion, upon which, for many reasons, it is impossible to depend. The opinion of friends is, needless to say, partial, whereas strangers will certainly not berate his works to his face, even though they may deserve it.
>
> When Canto Seven of *Onegin* came out, the journals, in general, reported on it very unfavorably. I would have readily believed them, had not their verdict clashed so inordinately with what they had said about the earlier chapters of my novel. After the excessive and undeserved praise that they lavished on the six parts of the very same work, I found it odd to hear, for example, the following critique.

Here Pushkin intended to give excerpts from Bulgarin's nasty attack in the *Northern Bee*, nos. 35 and 39: "Can we demand the public's attention to such compositions as, for example, Chapter Seven of *Eugene Onegin*? We thought at first that this was some mystification, merely a joke or a parody. . . . Not one idea in this watery Chapter Seven, not one sentiment, not one picture worthy of contemplation! A complete comedown, *chute complète*." Bulgarin also wrote "On p. 13 we find with a sense of the greatest enjoyment two stanzas omitted by the author himself and replaced with two beautiful numbers, VIII and IX."

Pushkin himself continued: "In one of our journals it was said that Chapter Seven could not have any success because the age and Russia go forward, whereas the author of the poem remains on the same spot. This verdict is unjust (i.e., in its conclusion). If the age may go forward, if sciences, philosophy, and civilization may perfect themselves and change, poetry remains stationary, it neither ages nor changes. Its goal, its means remain the same. . . . The works of true poets remain ever fresh and young." Pushkin also outlined an answer to Bulgarin's "review" in "Refutation of Criticism," but although his "hands itched to crush Bulgarin," he made no public reply.

***Chapter Eight* (SPb., 1832). First edition.**

In the foreword to this separate edition of the novel's final chapter, begun on Christmas Eve 1829 and revised and completed in the summer of 1831 ("Onegin's Letter" was composed on 5 October 1831), Pushkin noted: "The author frankly admits that he omitted a whole chapter from his novel, in which Onegin's journey through Russia was described. It rested with him whether this omitted chapter should be indicated by dots or by the numbering; but he decided that to avoid ambiguity he would better place number eight, not number nine, over the last chapter of *Eugene Onegin*." Byron's famous lines "Fare thee well, and if for ever, / Still for ever, fare thee well." served as the chapter's motto.

37

ASP, Eugene Onegin. First collected edition.

***Evgenii Onegin*. St. Petersburg, 1833.**

Kilgour 877.2

"Regarding the complete editions of 1833 and 1837 there reigns a rather eerie silence in his correspondence" (Nabokov). Pushkin referred to the "second edition," i.e., the first complete edition, published around 23 March 1833, in only one letter, to Pavel Nashchokin (1801–54): "Let this be my justification for my unpunctuality. When I arrived here [Petersburg] I found great disorders in my house; I have been compelled to discharge servants, to change cooks, and finally to rent a new apartment, and consequently to use sums which would otherwise have remained untouched. I hope that you have now received, kind Pavel Voinovich, the necessary papers for the remortgaging, and that you will receive the mortgage money without any difficulty. . . . You will receive the remainder of the debt in January—for I have already made arrangements, by selling to Smirdin the second edition of *Onegin*" (2 December 1832). Pushkin received 12,000 rubles for publication rights to this first complete edition; he had already earned 25,000 rubles for the separate chapters of the novel.

38

ASP, Eugene Onegin. Second collected edition.

***Evgenii Onegin*. St. Petersburg, 1837.**

Kilgour 877.3

The second complete edition, published by Il'ia Glazunov at the very end of December 1836 in a printing of 5,000 copies, is considered very rare: it sold out quickly after Pushkin's death on 29 January. Judging by the example of the pocket-sized edition in the Kilgour collection, bound in leather with moiré silk doublures, some copies had the fourth leaf, with the prefatory verse piece ("Not thinking to amuse . . .") to Pletnev, misplaced between pp. 204 (ending on Seven, II, 9) and 205. Volume Four of Nabokov's translation of the novel contains a photographic reproduction of this edition, the final one supervised by Pushkin. It is virtually identical with that of 1833.

· VI ·

BORIS GODUNOV

Both history and tragedy stood very high in prestige according to the system of literary values that had prevailed in Pushkin's youth. But Pushkin's own encounter with the autocratic government, his friends' involvement in the political conspiracies that culminated in the Decembrist uprising (14 December 1825), the experience of history-in-the-making that the Napoleonic era had given to all of Europe, and the powerful stimuli to thought and creativity that he encountered in Karamzin's *History*, in Shakespeare, and in contemporary European writing all contributed to the speed, intensity, and excitement with which he himself turned to historical drama.

Boris Godunov, completed in a year's work at Mikhailovskoe, challenged literary conventions, generic expectations, and official pieties no less daringly than had the narrative poems or *Eugene Onegin*. Its overwhelming wealth of scenes and settings (23 and 20, respectively), its play with received ideas about the protagonist's function in a historical drama, its incorporation of features from lyric poetry and the historical novel, its audacious distancing of the main characters, its treatment of the Pretender as an inspired creator, and its provocative contrast of Counter-Reformation Poland with medieval Moscovy all insured that it would provoke more puzzlement, envy, and hostility than admiration on the part of its contemporary critics. That the drama's behind-the-scenes censor, Bulgarin, helped to retard its publication for six years, plagiarized it before it was published, and then attacked it in his widely circulated periodicals did not contribute to its popularity. But at least Bulgarin's desperate actions show he understood the threat that Pushkin's *Boris* posed. A hundred and fifty years of reading, research, and interpretation have still not exhausted the depths and implications of Pushkin's own favorite text.

W M T

39

N. M. Karamzin,
History of the Russian state.

Istoriia gosudarstva rossiiskogo, v. 10–11. Petersburg, 1824.

Kilgour 495

If they [the government] will leave me in peace," Pushkin wrote to Zhukovsky in April 1825, "then probably I shall think only of unrhymed pentameters." Pushkin alludes to his blank verse play *Boris Godunov*, begun in November 1824 and resumed in the spring of 1825. He had been carefully reading Shakespeare (in French translation) and the latest volumes (X–XI) of Karamzin's *History*, and had found in the figure of the tormented Tsar, a historical character whose conflict with the Pretender Dmitrii fascinated writers all over Europe, a perfect subject for his radical rethinking of tragic dramatic form. When Viazemsky asked him for an outline of the play, he replied "You want a *plan*? Take the end of the tenth and all the eleventh volume, and there's a *plan* for you" (13 and 15 September 1825), and he had written of Karamzin's work to Zhukovsky: "What a marvel these last two volumes of Karamzin's are! What life! *C'est palpitant comme la gazette d'hier*" (17 August 1825).

He completed the play on 7 November 1825, and wrote to Viazemsky: "I congratulate you, *mon cher*, on the birth of a romantic tragedy, in which the principal personage is Boris Godunov! My tragedy is finished; I reread it aloud to myself and clapped my hands and shouted, 'at a boy, Pushkin, 'at a boy, you son of a bitch! . . . Zhukovsky says that the Tsar [Alexander I] will pardon me as a result of my tragedy — I doubt it, my dear fellow!"

Pushkin had to wait many years before seeing what he always called his favorite work in print. It then bore the dedication: "Inspired by his genius, Aleksandr Pushkin dedicates this work with veneration and gratitude to the memory of Nikolai Mikhailovich Karamzin, precious to Russians." Volume XI is open to Karamzin's account of the death of Boris and his musings on what were Boris's thoughts at that moment.

40

Baron A. A. Del'vig and Orest Somov (1793–1833), *editors*, Northern flowers for 1828.

***Severnye tsvety na 1828 god.* St. Petersburg, 1827.**

Kilgour 1049

On 3 September 1826, Pushkin was granted permission to leave Mikhailovskoe and was ordered to present himself to the new Tsar, Nicholas I, in Moscow. He met the Emperor in the Kremlin on 8 September, where Nicholas announced that from then on he would act as Pushkin's personal censor. Little did Pushkin realize that his fate was now in the hands of an uncomprehending, rather dim-witted reader who would show himself utterly capricious in his understanding of the "agreement" over the years to come. On 9 November 1826, Pushkin wrote to Iazykov: "The Tsar has freed me from the censorship. He himself is my censor. The advantage, of course, is immense. Thus shall we get *Godunov* into print." His hopes were quickly dashed.

In September and October Pushkin had read the play three times to the enthusiastic reception of his friends in Moscow, little dreaming that he should have asked for Imperial permission before doing so. On 22 November, Count Aleksandr Benckendorff, head of the Third Section of His Majesty's Private Chancery (the secret police) and the intermediary between Nicholas and the poet for the rest of

his life, wrote Pushkin and called him on the carpet for this temerity. He demanded that Pushkin send the play immediately for review. Pushkin complied on 29 November. The play was shown to Faddei Bulgarin, who made notes on it and wrote a review which Nicholas used for the comment Benckendorff forwarded to the author on 14 December 1826: "I consider that Mr. Pushkin's goal would be fulfilled if, along with necessary expurgations, he would recast his comedy into a historical tale or novel, similar to Walter Scott's." Pushkin politely replied on 3 January 1827: "It is with feelings of the most profound gratitude that I received Your Excellency's letter informing me of His Majesty's most gracious comment regarding my dramatic poem. I agree that it resembles a historical novel rather than a tragedy, as the Sovereign Emperor deigned to observe. I regret that I have not the power to recast what I have once written." Pushkin's decision kept the play, whose text was returned with offending passages marked by Nicholas, off the stage throughout his life and delayed publication by years.

A fragment of the play ("Night. A Cell in the Chudov Monastery"—ironically, where Pushkin's Kremlin interview with the Tsar had taken place) first appeared in *The Moscow Messenger*, Part One, No, 1, 1827. Del'vig published another ("1604. 16 October. The Lithuanian Border") in his almanac on 22 December 1827.

41

Mikhail Aleksandrovich Maksimovich (1804-73), ***editor,*** **The Dawn : an almanac for 1830.**

Dennitsa : almanakh na 1830 god.
Moscow, 1830.

Kilgour 264

Mikhail Maksimovich published the "First Two Scenes from the Tragedy Boris Godunov" in his almanac on 9 January 1830. The Kilgour copy is inscribed by the editor-publisher to Princess Zinaida Volkonskaia.

42

ASP, ***Boris Godunov.***

St. Petersburg, 1831.

Kilgour 884 (two copies)

In 1829 Pushkin tried without success to gain the Tsar's permission to publish *Boris*. On 7 January and 16 April 1830 he again wrote to Benckendorff about the matter, explaining that the sale of the play would help put his finances in order and thus help him press his proposal to Natalia Goncharova. On 28 April Nicholas, as a kind of "engagement present" agreed (Pushkin's letter to his parents of 3 May), and Pushkin wrote to Pletnev: "Dear fellow! Victory! The Tsar is permitting me to publish *Godunov* in its pristine beauty. Here is what Benckendorff writes me: Pour ce qui regarde votre tragédie de Godounof, Sa Majesté vous permet de la faire imprimer sous votre propre responsabilité" (ca. 5 May). Pletnev saw to all the publishing details (Pushkin received 10,000 rubles), and the play, with three omitted scenes, many censored lines, and a different ending from the one Pushkin had originally written, appeared for sale at the end of December 1830.

Pushkin worried that the public would fail to understand the play and in "Refutation of Criticism" predicted "My tragedy will probably have no success at all. The journals are angry with me. I lack the chief attractions as far as the public is concerned: youth and the novelty of a new literary name." He wrote several draft prefaces for the play in 1829–30, all based on ideas first expressed in letters to Nikolai Raevsky (the first, a rough draft never sent, of July 1825; the second, also

БОРИСЪ ГОДУНОВЪ,

СОЧИНЕНІЕ

АЛЕКСАНДРА ПУШКИНА.

САНКТПЕТЕРБУРГЪ.

1831.

No. 42

a rough draft and also in French, of 30 January or 30 June 1829). In the second letter to Raevsky, he wrote:

> Following Shakespeare's example, I confine myself to describing an epoch and historical characters, without digging for theatrical effect, Romantic pathos, etc.. . . . The style is mixed — it is common and low where I was obliged to bring on vulgar, coarse characters. . . . A tragedy without love beckoned to [*souriait à*] my imagination. But apart from the fact that love has a large role to play in the romantic, passionate character of my adventurous hero, I made Dmitrii in love with Marina in order to bring out her strange character the better. Karamzin has still only sketched it, but indeed it's a funny sort of fine woman. She has only one passion, ambition, but to such a height of energy and rage that one can scarce conceive it. . . . In writing my Godunov, I puzzled about tragedy, and if I ever set about making a preface on the subject, I would raise a scandal — it is, perhaps, the least understood of genres. They have tried to found its laws on probability, and probability is just what the nature of drama forbids — not to speak of time, place, etc., what the devil has probability to do with a room cut in two, one half of which is occupied by 2,000 persons, supposedly invisible to those who trip the boards . . .? True tragic geniuses have never meddled with any probability but that of character and situation.

As Pushkin feared, the play (without any preface) enjoyed no success with readers or critics, and certainly failed to "influence the reform of Russian dramatic art," as he had hoped it would. It is probably best known from the work of another radical reformer, Modest Mussorgsky, who based his innovative opera of the same title on Pushkin and a rereading of Karamzin. The play can still arouse controversy, and the banning of Iurii Liubimov's production at Moscow's Taganka Theater in 1982 shows that the political potential of the play has not lessened in our day.

A bound copy of the play (with the bookplate of Grand Duke Constantine Nikolaevich) is open to the dedication to Karamzin. Another copy, with the original wrappers, is from the Princess Volkonskaia collection.

43

F. V. Bulgarin, Le faux Démétrius, ou, L'Imposteur : roman historique / traduit du russe par Victor Fleury. 4 v.

St. Petersburg, Paris, 1832.

The notorious police informer and cutthroat journalist Bulgarin is most popularly remembered for his venomous attacks on Pushkin, which began with a grossly insulting "Anecdote" in *The Northern Bee* on 12 March 1830 (No. 30) and continued right up to Pushkin's death. They provoked some of Pushkin's most devastating epigrams and satires, in several of which he dubbed him "Figliarin" (Bulgarin was a Pole; the Russian *figliar*, meaning "mountebank, buffoon," comes from the Polish *figlarz.*) The depth of their enmity is well shown by the Post Scriptum to Pushkin's "My Genealogy," an ironical poem on his ancestry written in reply to Bulgarin's "reprehensible provocation", "The Second Letter from Karlovo to Kamennyi Ostrov" (August 1830); Pushkin concludes his P.S.: "Inspired Figliarin has decided: I am a bourgeois nobleman. But what is he in his highly-respected family? He? he is a Bourgeois Street nobleman [literally "A nobleman on Meshchanskaia [Bourgeois] Street," Petersburg's red-light district]." Bulgarin had married a former prostitute and niece of a brothel-keeper.

Ever conscious of publicity, Bulgarin courted foreign visitors to Russia, such as the French poet and dramatist Jacques-Arsène Ancelot (1794–1854). Pushkin alluded to this (without naming Bulgarin) in "Fragments of Letters, Thoughts, and Comments" (*Northern Flowers for 1828*): "The traveller Ancelot speaks [in *Six mois en Russie*, 1827] of some grammar [Grech's], yet unpublished, that ratifies the rules of our language; of some novel [Bulgarin's], still in manuscript, that has made its

No.43:
Bulgarin (from no. 58)

author famous. . . . What an amusing literature!" Bulgarin's shameless self-promotion was obviously successful, given the quick translation into French of his *Dimitrii the Pretender* (1830).

Pushkin recognized the novel's plagiarism of his own still unpublished play. Bulgarin had helped censor the work and tried to block its publication for six years.

44

Aleksei Stepanovich Khomiakov (1804–60), Dimitrii the Pretender.

Dimitrii samozvanets : tragediia v piati deistviiakh. **Moscow, 1833.**

Kilgour 513

Pushkin's generically innovative text could not spawn imitations, but it did provoke several polemical replies from authors who disagreed with his perspective on the "Time of Troubles." Khomiakov's Slavophile treatment is open to a passage which shows its transparent dependency on Pushkin, as Dimitrii "recalls the green twilight of the gardens, the allée of limetrees and the plashing fountain . . ." where he met with Marina Mniszek. He is "remembering" only the Garden Scene ("Night. A Garden. A Fountain") of Pushkin's original: there is no historical evidence for the encounter and nothing about it in Karamzin.

45

Mikhail Evstaf'evich Lobanov (1787–1846),

Boris Godunov : tragediia v trekh deistviiakh.
St. Petersburg, 1835.

Kilgour 649

Lobanov's wretched "tragedy in three acts" is open to its "To the Reader," which clearly announces the author's monarchist viewpoint: "The tempests which shook Russia during the reigns of crowned heads not of the blood of St. Vladimir and which smashed them, were calmed only by the selection of a legitimate Sovereign [i.e., Mikhail Romanov]." In "M. E. Lobanov's Opinion of the Spirit of Literature, Both Abroad and at Home" (*The Contemporary*, III 1836, unsigned), Pushkin gave a reasoned answer to Lobanov's address to the Russian Academy on 18 January 1836, and disputed his "absurd" comments on the censorship: "Let us close with the sincere wish that the Russian Academy . . . will punish the undeserving by its sole proper weapon: paying them no attention."

46

Kondratii Fedorovich Ryleev (1795–1826), Meditations.

Dumy.
Moscow, 1825.

Kilgour 994

Ryleev dreamed of liberating the Russian people from autocracy and, like many of his heroes, died a martyr, executed on 13 July 1826 for his central role in the Decembrist rebellion. He used the verse genre known as the *duma*, a short historical poem, to celebrate heroes of Russia's past, usually those who died in the name of some glorious cause. His collection, open to Meditation 13, a character sketch-monologue of Boris Godunov, a conscience-stricken monarch chosen to represent the spirit of his tumultuous age, appeared at the time Pushkin was at work on Boris. He was unsparing in his criticism when he wrote to Ryleev (pointing at just those things he wanted to avoid in his own play): "What shall I say to you about

ДУМЫ.

Сочиненіе К. Рылѣева.

Гр. Ал. Флоровъ.

Москва.
Въ Типографіи С. Селивановскаго.
1825.

the *Dumy*? Vivid lines are to be met in all of them . . . but on the whole they are all weak in invention and exposition. They are all cut to the same pattern, made up of *points in common* (*loci topici*): the description of the site of the action, the hero's speech, and—the moral. There is nothing national, nothing Russian in them at all, except the names" (second half of May 1825). He was categorical in a letter to Viazemsky of 25 May: "On the other hand, the *Dumy* are trash and the name comes from the German *dumm*, and not from the Polish, as it would seem at first glance [both word and genre were taken from Ukrainian]".

The Kilgour copy is bound with Ryleev's *Voinarovsky* (1825), a verse tale about a hero of Ukrainian nationalist aspirations, the nephew of the Hetman Mazeppa. Pushkin had kinder words for it, but polemicized with its view of Peter in *Poltava*.

47

Aleksandr Sergeevich Griboedov (1795–1829), Woe from wit.

Gore ot uma. (MS., ca. 1825).
———. Moscow, 1833.
———. (MS., 1839).
———. St. Petersburg, 1839.

Kilgour 404, 405 and 1335

Pushkin, like hundreds of others, first encountered Griboedov's masterpiece in manuscript. On 11 January 1825 his old Lycée chum Ivan Pushchin brought a copy of the four-act comedy, written between 1822–24 in freely rhymed iambic lines of varying length, to Mikhailovskoe. They spent the better part of their brief time together reading the play aloud. Shortly after, on 28 January, Pushkin outlined his reaction in a letter to Viazemsky: "I have read Chatsky [the play's hero]—there is much that is witty and amusing in the verses, but there is no plan, no main idea, no truth in the whole comedy. Chatsky is not at all an intelligent man, but Griboedov is very intelligent." At about the same time Pushkin developed his neoclassical strictures on the play in a letter to Aleksandr Bestuzhev. He admitted that he had listened to the play only once and not with the attention it deserved. "Traits of a truly comic genius" there were, but "In the comedy *Woe from Wit* who is the intelligent character? The answer: Griboedov. And do you know who Chatsky is? A fiery, noble, and fine fellow who has spent some time with a very intelligent man (namely with Griboedov) and has drunk his fill of his thoughts, witticisms, and satiric observations. Everything he says is very intelligent. But to whom does he say it all?. . . . Of the verses I shall say nothing: half of them are bound to become proverbs [an accurate prediction]. Show this to Griboedov. Perhaps I've erred in something. While I was listening to his comedy I was not criticizing, but enjoying myself."

Griboedov lived to see only a fragment of the play (scenes vii–x of Act I and the whole of Act III) published, in Bulgarin's collection *The Russian Thalia* ("a present for the male and female lovers of the fatherland's theater for 1825"), mid-December 1824 (also in the Kilgour collection). On 30 January 1829, while serving as Russia's ambassador to Persia, he was killed and his body mutilated when a mob attacked the Russian legation in Teheran. In Chapter Two of "A Journey to Erzerum" Pushkin described meeting the cart bringing Griboedov's body from Teheran for burial in Tiflis, and he recalled his "melancholy character" and "embittered intelligence," adding "His comedy, *Woe from Wit*, still in manuscript, produced an indescribable impression, and suddenly placed him on a level with our foremost poets."

Parts of Act I were staged in Petersburg in 1829. Other fragmentary performances followed before the first reasonably complete one, given 26 January 1831. The censorship permitted publication of a heavily cut and altered version in 1833, the same year as the first complete edition of *Eugene Onegin*, in which there are several references to the play. Another text appeared in 1839, with a hundred-page recollection of the author by Ksenofon Polevoi (1801–67). Only in 1862 was a more or less complete text allowed to be printed.

In the meantime thousands of manuscript copies circulated throughout the Empire. Soviet archives contain over four hundred such texts. As early as 1830 Bulgarin could state: "There is now not a single small town, nor a house where

ДѢЙСТВІЕ II.

ЯВЛЕНІЕ I.

Фамусовъ и Слуга.

Фамусовъ.

Петрушка вѣчно ты съ обновкой,
Съ разорваннымъ локтемъ! Достань-ка календарь,
Читай, не такъ, какъ пономарь,
А съ чувствомъ, съ толкомъ, съ растановкой.
Постой-же. На листѣ черкни, на записномъ.
Противу будущей недѣли:
Къ Прасковьѣ Ѳедоровнѣ въ домъ,
Во вторникъ званъ я на форели.
Куда какъ чуденъ созданъ свѣтъ!
Пофилософствуй - умъ вскружится!
То бережешься, то обѣдъ;
Ѣшь три часа, а въ три дни не сварится!
Отмѣть-ка, въ тотъ же день.... нѣтъ, нѣтъ......
Въ четвергъ, я званъ на погребенье.
Охъ, родъ людской! Пришло въ забвенье,

they love literature, in which one could not find a copy of this comedy, unfortunately, disfigured by copyists." The Houghton Library possesses two such copies, one from the 1820's (Ms Russian 23.1), another dated 1839 (MS Russian 23), both on display here. The 1839 octavo copy is a particularly fine calligraphic example, with Title, headings, and stage directions in black India ink and the cursive text in brown. A former owner had manuscript leaves with suppressed passages bound into the elegant miniature 1839 edition. All four copies are open to Chatsky's famous monologue in Act II, scene v, from which the final twelve lines (384–95) were excised in the printed texts. The first English translation, by Nicholas Benardaky (London, 1857; also in the Kilgour collection), rendered them in prose: "All their respect is reserved for the uniform alone, which, in former times, concealed under its embroidered trappings the cowardice and imbecility of their natures, and they beckon *us* to follow them on the same glorious path. Their wives and daughters are victims of the same passion. It is not long since I felt something of the same childish admiration, for I was carried away by the common impulse. You must remember when some of the guardsmen arrived in Moscow on a short visit, that all the women rent the air with acclamations, and threw up their caps in applause." The "freeness" of the translation suggests that Benardaky relied on a very faulty copy of the text.

· VII ·

THE PUSHKIN PLÉIADE

The poets represented in this case were Pushkin's schoolfellows at the Imperial Lycée (Del'vig, Kiukhel'beker), fellow members of the playful Arzamas literary society (Viazemsky, Davydov), or poets whom Pushkin befriended as they came to prominence in the late 1810's and 1820's (Baratynsky, Kozlov, Iazykov). More important, they were among the most luminous stars in the so-called "Pushkin Pléiade," a term which derives from the epistle dedicatory in Baratynsky's magisterial collection *Twilight* (*Sumerki*). Appropriately enough, Baratynsky first published this epistle to Viazemsky in a journal that Pushkin founded, *The Contemporary*. At one time or another Pushkin enlisted most of these poets in his periodical enterprises—*The Literary Gazette*, *Northern Flowers for 1832*, or *The Contemporary*—or else helped them to publish their works separately. He reviewed them with unfailing generosity in these same periodicals.

The poets of the Pléiade wrote many verse epistles to each other, in which they demonstrated the differences and similarities in their poetic styles. They enjoyed their greatest popularity as poets in the 1820's, although by the end of the decade their ties of respect and friendly rivalry had provoked hostile charges of "aristocratism" on the part of such writer-journalists as Bulgarin, Grech, and Nikolai Polevoi, who strove to replace them on fashion's bookshelf and to turn the Golden Age of Russian poetry into an age of prose. The poets of the Pléiade, including Pushkin himself, wrote many of their finest lyrics during the 1830's, when the attention of many Russian readers had turned toward prose fiction, history, and journalism.

W M T

48

Baron A. A. Del'vig, Poems.

Stikhotvoreniia. St. Petersburg, 1829.

Kilgour 259

The modest Del'vig, first among Pushkin's friends from their days in the first class of the Lycée, wrote little and published less. The fashionable pose of "poetic laziness" was a fact with this indolent and kind-hearted man, who attracted the friendship of the finest writers of the day. Aided by his comrades from the "literary aristocrats," he founded and edited the distinguished almanac *Northern Flowers*, and *The Literary Gazette*. Pushkin was stunned by the news of his death: "It is sad, heartbreaking. This is the first death I have ever wept over. . . . Nobody in the world was closer to me than Del'vig. . . . Without him we are as though orphaned" (to Pletnev, 21 January 1831). In the draft for an article about the poet (written not later than 1834 and published posthumously), Pushkin praised the "vivacity of his imagination" and his "uncommon feeling for harmony and that classical proportion to which he was never unfaithful." Pushkin concluded: "he was not appreciated at his early appearance in his short-lived career; and he is still not appreciated now, when he lies at rest in his premature grave!"

"By a marvelous coincidence, Del'vig died on the anniversary of the death of the fictional Lensky (who is compared to him here [*Onegin*] on the eve of a fatal duel); and the wake commemorating Del'vig's death was held by his friends (Pushkin, Viazemsky, Baratynsky, Iazykov) in a Moscow restaurant on 27 January 1831, exactly six years before Pushkin's fatal duel" (*Nabokov*).

49

E. A. Baratynsky, Eda : a Finnish tale ; and The feasts : a descriptive long poem.

Eda : finliandskaia povest' ; i Piry : opisatel'naia poema. **St. Petersburg, 1826.**

Kilgour 100

When he sent a copy of the book (published 1 February, 1826) to Praskoviia Osipova on 20 February 1826, Pushkin described *Eda* as a "*chef-d'oeuvre de grâce, d'élégance et de sentiment*," testimony to his loyalty to an old friend rather than to his discrimination in this case. The revised 1826 text of *The Feasts*, a nostalgic evocation of friendly gatherings in Petersburg in 1819, written in 1820 and first published in 1821, is open to lines 185–91 [ll. 178–83 of the revised text of 1835], addressed to Pushkin.

Our P. . .n, you to whom 'tis given
to sing heroes and wine,
wild passions and an escapade,
who with a prankish mind can blend
a wondrous knowledge of the heart,
and who can be (not a small thing, meseems!)
most amiable at table.
(Nabokov transl.)

The poem also hailed the "volatile and wise Pushkin" as the "enchanting bard of love, liberty, and pleasure."

Pushkin repaid the compliment by saluting Baratynsky as "the bard of *The Feasts* and languid melancholy" in *Eugene Onegin* (Three, XXX, 1) and by using one of its lines as a motto for the "Moscow chapter" (Seven) of *Onegin*, "How can one not love one's native Moscow?"

50

E. A. Baratynsky, Poems.

Stikhotvoreniia. **Moscow, 1827.**

Kilgour 101

Baratynsky's *Poems* was "regarded by Pushkin with a tender and grave respect: its tonality is unique in the annals of the greater poet's literary sympathies" (Nabokov). Pushkin sketched out, but did not publish, a review of the 1827 collection, divided into sections entitled "Elegies" ("Baratynsky's first works were elegies and he reigns supreme in this genre"), "Miscellany," and "Epistles." In 1830, during his seclusion at Boldino, Pushkin began a long article (left unfinished and published posthumously) that begins with the following well-known evaluation of his fellow poet: "Baratynsky belongs to the number of our excellent poets. He is original among us in that he thinks. He would be original everywhere since he thinks in his own way, justly and independently, and at the same time feels intensely and deeply. The harmony of his verses, the freshness of his style, the liveliness and precision of his expression, must astonish anyone having the least measure of taste and sensibility."

The Kilgour collection also has his two-volume *Poems* (1835), with a frontispiece portrait, and the great *Twilight* (*Sumerki*), the first collection of a major Russian poet with a thematic rather than generic title or the simple "Poems of . . . . "

Е: А: БАРАТЫНСКІЙ.

No.50: Baratynsky, from his Poems (1835)

51

Prince P. A. Viazemsky, Salutation to V. A. Zhukovsky, 29 January 1849.

Privetstvie V. A. Zhukovskomu, 29 ianvaria 1849 goda.
St. Petersburg, 1849.

Kilgour 1250

"He was Karamzin's ward, Reason's godchild, Romanticism's champion, and an Irishman on his mother's side (O'Reilly)" (Nabokov), and one of Pushkin's oldest and most loyal friends. He was the first reader and critic of many of Pushkin's works and provoked a large number of his most scintillating (at spots unprintable) letters. Pushkin respected his quick wit, trenchant criticism, and fine prose style more than his minor poetry. He deeply appreciated all that Viazemsky did for him and his fellow writers. Indeed, Viazemsky was forced to retire from his last bureaucratic post—head of the censorship—for insufficient strictness. He outlived all his friends, and survived into an often embittered old age to become the apologist of his early literary milieu.

Viazemsky, unlike Pushkin, could afford to take a "gentlemanly" attitude toward the publication of his works because of a substantial private income. He participated in all the major almanacs and selected "respectable" periodicals of his day, but had no need to bring out a collected edition of his verse or prose. Twelve volumes appeared only in 1878–96. The unbound brochure on display here, an offprint from the newspaper *The Russian Invalid* (No. 23), now seems a rather anachronistic relic of the sentimentalist cult of enthusiastic friendship widespread in Viazemsky's circle in the early decades of the century. The text, written for a celebration organized by Viazemsky for some eighty people in Petersburg, commemorates Zhukovsky's sixty-sixth birthday and fifty years of his literary activity. It was sent to him in Baden-Baden.

52

Ivan Ivanovich Kozlov (1779–1840), The monk : a Kievan tale.

Chernets : kievskaia povest'. **St. Petersburg, 1825.**

Kilgour 556

All his friends, Pushkin among them, deeply respected the courage and moral strength with which the gentle Kozlov endured crippling physical pain and finally blindness. He taught himself to read and write English, and the "Russian Byron," as he was popularly called for works like *The Monk* (with its four-line epigraph from *The Giaour*), translated *The Bride of Abydos* into Russian (1826; in the Kilgour collection).

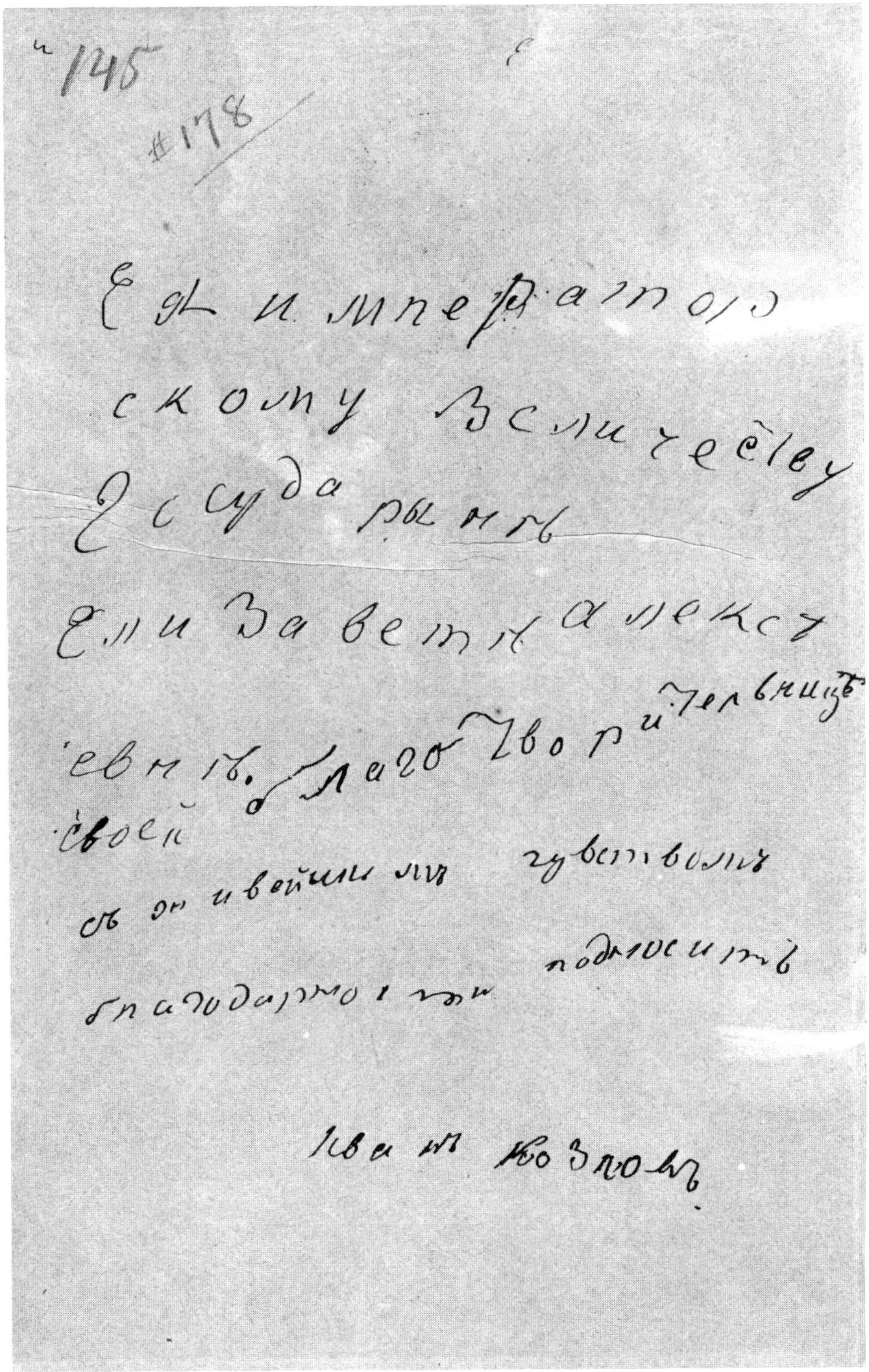
145
#178
Ея Императорскому Величеству
Государынѣ
Елизаветѣ Алексеевнѣ благотворительницѣ
своей
съ почтительнымъ чувствомъ
благодарности подноситъ
Иванъ Козловъ.

The Monk, the tale of a young monk with a dark past, also contained an epistle to Kozlov's tireless benefactor, Zhukovsky ("To my friend V. A. Zh."). In the first half of May 1825, Pushkin, to whom Kozlov had sent a graciously inscribed copy, wrote to his brother: "The blind poet's signature touched me inexpressibly. His tale is charming. . . . The epistle is perhaps better than the poem itself — at least the terrible place where the poet describes how he became blind will remain forever the epitome of the poetry of agony."

The Kilgour copy is open to Kozlov's barely legible inscription of the volume to the Empress Elizaveta Alekseevna, wife of Alexander I. Book stamp of the Imperial Library of Tsarskoe Selo.

53

Denis Vasil'evich Davydov (1784–1839), Poems.

***Stikhotvoreniia.* Moscow, 1832**

Kilgour 257

This "hussar-poet" celebrant of vodka, women, and song had modest gifts and a great talent for self-promotion, which he played to the hilt. Tolstoy used him as the model for Denisov in War and Peace. Pushkin knew him since their escapades together in the "Arzamasian Society of Obscure People" in the late teens, and liked the conversational manner and high spirits of his verse. Davydov sent Pushkin a personal copy of this collection.

Davydov's fame as a partisan hero of the war against the French (1812–14) could not protect him from the caprice of the censorship, as Pushkin found out when he published his "Of Partisan Warfare" in the third issue of *The Contemporary* in 1836. In August he wrote Davydov: "I do not know what wrong has been done by Russian writers, who are not only meek, but are even themselves in accord with the spirit of the government. But I do know that they have never been so oppressed as now: not even in the last five years of the reign of the late Emperor, when all literature remained in manuscript. . . ."

54

Nikolai Mikhailovich Iazykov (1803–47), Poems.

***Stikhotvoreniia*.**
St. Petersburg, 1833

Kilgour 451

Pushkin called him "inspired Iazykov" in *Eugene Onegin* (Four, XXXI,9) and enthusiastically greeted the "intoxication" of his verse. They met in the summer of 1826 when Iazykov visited Pushkin's country neighbors the Osipovs at Trigorskoe, their country estate. Pushkin's 1826 "To Iazykov" salutes those qualities most admired by his contemporaries: "Iazykov, who inspired you / with your dashing message? / How mischievous, how dear you are / what an abundance of feelings and strengths, what youthful ebullience!" In an unsigned review of the *Nevsky Almanac for 1830* (in *The Literary Gazette*, No. 12, 1830) Pushkin wrote: "The poetry section is graced by Iazykov. From the moment he first appeared, this poet has astonished us by the fire and force of his language. No one has more authoritative control of cadence and phrasing. It seems there is no subject whose poetic side he could not grasp and express with that vividness so characteristic of him. We regret that so far he has scarcely gone beyond the limits of one overly narrow genre . . . ."

Poems is open to the passage of "Trigorskoe," one of his best poems, in which, rather absurdly, he puts himself on equal poetic footing with Pushkin, but also provides some glimpses of his life in the country. His 1826 "To Pushkin" was published only after the older poet's death, as was an 1827 poem addressed to Mme. Osipova, in which he described "our famous Pushkin" as "Voltaire, Racine, and Goethe, all in one."

55

Vil'gel'm Karlovich Kiukhel'beker (Küchelbecker) (1797–1846), Izhorsky : a mystery play.

***Izhorsky : misteriia*.**
St. Petersburg, 1835.

Kilgour 520

Pushkin respected the high political ideals of this ardent Russian patriot of German descent; the literary views of the "stern critic" of *Eugene Onegin* (Four, XXXII, 1) were another matter. In "On the Tendency of Our Poetry, Especially in the Last Decade," published in the almanac *Mnemosyne*, pt. II (1824) which he and Prince Vladimir Odoevsky (1803–69) edited, Kiukhel'beker criticized the Russian elegy for triteness and vagueness and held up the ode as a model of inspired lyricism. Pushkin received his due in the article ("When one reads any elegy by Zhukovsky, Pushkin, or Baratynsky, everything is familiar. . . . The images are everywhere the same"), and alluded to it in the foreword to the separate edition of Chapter One of Eugene Onegin (1825).

After his arrest for participation in the Decembrist revolt, Kiukhel'beker spent ten years of imprisonment in various fortresses and died in Siberian exile. Pushkin left a moving account in his diary of his chance encounter with his old schoolmate, who was being moved from Schlüsselburg fortress to the Dinaburg fortress, on 15 October 1827. The exaggerated enthusiasms of "Kiukhlia" often provoked Pushkin's good-hearted sarcasm:

"Kiukhel'beker writes me in tetrameters that he has been in Germany, in Paris, in the Caucasus, and that he has been falling off his horse. All that is *à propos A Prisoner of the Caucasus*" (to Gnedich, 13 May 1823). Pushkin always thought him a bit of a crank and had little use for his "archaizing" verse: "What an odd fellow!

Only he could have gotten into his head the Jewish notion of lauding Greece — magnificent, classical, poetic Greece, Greece, where everything breathes of mythology and heroism — in Slavonic-Russian verses taken wholesale from Jeremiah" (to Lev Pushkin, 4 September 1822). But Pushkin did everything in his power after 1826 to try to print Kiukhel'beker's works. Thanks to his considerable efforts, parts one and two of the highly original *Izhorsky* were printed anonymously in 1835 "In the Third Section of H. I. M. Personal Chancery," i.e., by the secret police.

The Kilgour copy formerly belonged to the well-known Pushkinist Nikolai Lerner and contains a note in his hand about the publication history of the play.

JOURNALISM, PROSE, AND THE "AGE OF SMIRDIN"

Two forms of literary activity, journalism and prose fiction, came to the fore at the end of the 1820's, challenging the hegemony that the poets of the decade had enjoyed on the Russian literary scene. The materials in this case display the contributions of Aleksandr Smirdin (temporarily successful) and Aleksandr Pushkin (a commercial failure) to the dissemination of these new forms, which many Russians saw, for better or worse, as central to the development of a modern institution of literature.

The 1820's and 1830's witnessed two interrelated developments in Russian journalism: (1) the rise of commercially viable periodicals (the almanacs in the 1820's and the "encyclopedic" journals in the 1830's); (2) a shift in the orientation of the literary criticism in these periodicals from the sort that would be helpful to writers preparing their texts to the sort that would entertain and form a reading public. Toward the beginning of the period Prince Viazemsky could justly scorn Russian periodicals—"all our journals are school archives of pupils' essays." But by 1840 the most popular critic among the younger generation, Vissarion Belinsky, could no less persuasively place periodical literature at the very center of Russian literary life: "the journal has now swallowed up our entire literature—the public doesn't want books, it wants journals, and in the journals they publish whole plays and novels, and each issue of the journal weighs forty pounds."

Despite unscrupulous competitive tactics by Russian journalists, government interference, feckless management by the publishers, and frequent disrespect on the part of reluctant gentlemen-contributors, the periodical press became a medium for the discussion of important cultural controversies (literary language, 1800's–1840's; literary "aristocratism," 1828–31; literary commerce, 1835-36) and began, haltingly, to serve a cultural situation in which writer and reader no longer faced each other across a Moscow or Petersburg drawing room. Belinsky mocked the fodder that the most successful of the journals, *The Library For Reading*, cast before its readers: "The daughter reads the verses of Messrs Ershov, Gorniev, Strugovshchikov and the stories of Messrs Zagoskin, Ushakov, Panaev, Kalashnikov, and Masal'sky; the son, as a member of the new generation, reads the verses of Mr. Timofeev and the stories of Baron Brambeus; papa reads articles about the two- and three-field systems, about various means of fertilizing the land; and mamma reads about a new way of curing coughs and dyeing thread"—but neither Belinsky, nor Gogol, nor Pushkin could deny the role that Smirdin's editor, Osip Ivanovich Senkovsky, played in shaping public opinion.

WMT

56

Aleksandr Filippovich Smirdin (1795-1857),
Inventory of Russian books for reading from the library of Aleksandr Smirdin : arranged in systematic order.

Rospis' rossiiskim knigam dlia chteniia, iz biblioteki Aleksandra Smirdina : sistematicheskim poriadkom raspolozhennaia. 4 pts.
St. Petersburg, 1828.

Kilgour 1095

In 1817, the twenty-two year old Aleksandr Smirdin moved to Petersburg from Moscow, where he had served as an apprentice in a small bookshop, to work for the bookseller Vasilii Plavil'shchikov. In less than ten years he had inherited the business and made the subscription library bearing his name the largest and most popular in the northern capital. The 9,934 entries of his *Inventory* are divided into

No.56: Smirdin's "Housewarming" (from no. 57)

"four parts, with the addition of an Alphabetical List of the names of the authors and translators, and a Short List of books in alphabetical order" (a long-winded way of saying there are two indexes). These are further subdivided into twenty-three large headings, of which the first is "Theology" and the last a supplement to the index. Bringing up the rear are five categories (XVIII–XXII) of *belles-lettres*, a neat indication of literature's status at the time.

Subscribers could borrow (or buy) seven of Pushkin's works, all in section XX ("Literary Works in Verse"—*Proizvedeniia slovesnosti piiticheskiia*), divided into many categories and subcategories ("Works of one author," "Epic verse," "Romantic narrative poems," etc.). Use of the library was by no means cheap: a yearly subscription cost thirty rubles, six months twenty rubles, three months twelve, one month five. If a reader wanted to borrow journals as well, he paid an additional twenty, twelve, seven, and five rubles for each category. The shorter-term subscriptions reflect Smirdin's awareness of the needs of landowners visiting the capital during "the season" and bureaucrats on official visits.

Also in the collection are four supplements to the inventory of Russian books, published in 1829, 1832, 1852, and 1856. The last two are entitled "Third [-Fourth] supplement to the Inventory of Russian books for reading, from the library of Petr Krasheninnikov. Sequel to the formerly published inventories of A. F. Smirdin." By the late 1840's, Smirdin's overextended and undercapitalized business had fallen into bankruptcy.

57

A. F. Smirdin, Housewarming.

Novosel'e. 2 pts.
St. Petersburg, 1833–34.

By the 1830's, Smirdin had so expanded his business—into publishing books, journals (the monthly *Library for Reading*, founded in 1834, Russia's first "thick journal" and the most successful periodical of the decade), miscellanies, print shop—as to acquire a virtual monopoly over the Russian booktrade. Belinsky recognized the fact by labelling the 1830's "the Age of Smirdin." In 1832, in a kind of symbolic affirmation of the triumph of his commercial network, Smirdin moved his successful establishment to a fashionable address on Nevsky Prospect (22–24, in a building belonging to the adjacent Lutheran Church of St. Peter). He celebrated the event with a "housewarming" to which he invited the most prominent writers of the day. Nikolai Grech, in a detailed account of the event in *The Northern Bee*, No. 45, put the number of guests at fifty-one; other accounts spoke of eighty, and as many as one hundred and twenty "brothers of the pen." He commemorated the occasion with two elegantly printed and expensive almanacs, filled with engravings by the finest Russian artists.

Part (Book) One is open to the frontispiece (the Kilgour copy lacks the title page), with Stepan Galaktionov's engraving after a sketch by the portraitist and architect Aleksandr Pavlovich Briullov (1798–1877); for decades the drawing was wrongly attributed to Karl Briullov, the most successful painter of the day. It shows a corner of the U-shaped table set up for the banquet on 19 February 1832. Smirdin himself stands behind Krylov, who sits massively at the head of the table. To his right are the poetaster Dmitrii Khvostov (1756–1835; a frequent figure of fun for Pushkin) and Pushkin. If Pushkin looks slightly bemused and distant, it can be explained not by the champagne bottle standing in front of him, but by the persons seated opposite, to the left of Krylov. Two of them were his most despised journalist antagonists: the unscrupulous polemicist Nikolai Grech (1787–1867), raising his glass, the censor Vasilii Semenov, and the hated Faddei Bulgarin, joint editor with Grech of *The Northern Bee*. At one point during the festivities Pushkin shouted across the table: "Brother Semenov, you're just like Christ on Golgotha today!"

No.57:
"The little house at Kolomna"—
ASP's sketch for an illustration (from no. 73) and Briullov's rendering of it

The almanac's first volume, in which prose and verse were mixed (with the table of contents listing each separately), contained verse by Krylov, Zhukovsky, Viazemsky, Kozlov, Gnedich, Khomiakov, Baratynsky ("On the Death of Goethe"), and the first publication of Pushkin's comic masterpiece "The Little House in Kolomna" ("*Domik v Kolomne*"), with an engraving after a drawing by A. P. Briullov.

Part Two of the almanac, containing the first publications of Pushkin's "Angelo" ("*Andzhelo,*" a verse narrative version of Measure for Measure) and Gogol's "Two Ivans" (signed only "Rudyi Pan'ko"), is open to the cover, with Galaktionov's engraving after a drawing by A. P. Sapozhnikov showing the interior of the bookshop, with Pushkin standing at the far right (a bad likeness).

58

A. F. Smirdin, *editor*, One hundred Russian littérateurs.

***Sto russkikh literatorov*. 3 v. (all published). St. Petersburg, 1839–45.**

Kilgour 1129

Smirdin always conceived projects on a grand scale. In the preface dated 12 February 1839 to the first volume (on display here), he explained that he planned ten volumes, each to contain first publications of ten authors, and that he hoped to issue at least one volume a year, if not more. As it turned out, only three volumes appeared and at great intervals. The series came to an end with his bankruptcy. But projects like this and his publishing of over seventy contemporary and eighteenth-century Russian authors in modestly priced editions helped to canonize a Russian literary tradition.

Volume One contains first publications, each with the author's engraved portrait and an illustration for the work, by Aleksandrov, Bestuzhev-Marlinsky, Davydov, Zotov, Kukol'nik, Nikolai Polevoi, Pushkin, Svin'in, Senkovsky ("Baron Brambeus," the editor of the *Library for Reading* and the most widely read journalist of the 1830's), and Shakhovskoi, a rather mind-boggling array for the literary historian. It is open to the first publication of Pushkin's "little tragedy" "The Stone Guest" and the facing engraving by A. P. Briullov. "One Chapter from an Unfinished Novel" [*"Gosti s"ezzhalis' na dachu* ***"] and a rather mediocre engraving after Kiprensky's portrait are also in the volume.

No.58: Smirdin's "Housewarming" (from no. 57)

59

Baron A. A. Del'vig, *editor*, The Literary gazette.

***Literaturnaia gazeta.* St. Petersburg, 1830–31.**

Diaghilev-Lifar library 522.

Pushkin and his friends, pressed from one side by hostile journalists like Bulgarin and Grech and from another by "new men" like Nikolai Polevoi, resentful of their "establishment" status (Pushkin called him a "shop clerk"), had long talked of founding a literary forum for their views and works. Bulgarin did everything he could to block the venture, but late in 1829, Del'vig, who had agreed to edit the periodical only if his friends would help him, received permission to publish. The first issue appeared on 1 January 1830. Until its demise, the publishers — Del'vig, Orest Somov, Viazemsky, Pushkin, and Zhukovsky (while the order reflects the intensity of collaboration in the actual editing, Pushkin and Viazemsky were the leading spirits) — tried to put out one issue every five days. The Gazette featured excellent verse (issue one contained a fragment from the Eighth Chapter of *Onegin*), prose fiction (Gogol), translations from Western literature (Tieck, Scott, Stendhal, Manzoni, E. T, A. Hoffmann, etc.), criticism, bibliographical notices, literary news, and lively, often wickedly pointed, polemics with its main opponents (Pushkin's portrait of the "scribbler-spy" Bulgarin, for example, thinly disguised as a review of the memoirs of the French police spy Vidocq in the twentieth issue). Even before it appeared, Bulgarin had received promises that a rival to his *Northern Bee* would be forbidden to publish political news of any kind, knowing that this would almost certainly assure failure for the enterprise. Pushkin realized the potential consequences when he wrote to Viazemsky on 2 May 1830: "The fact is that a purely literary gazette cannot exist among us; one must take as ally either Fashion or Politics. To compete with Raich and Shalikov [whose journals *Galatea* and *The Ladies' Journal* offered fashion news] is somehow shameful. But can it really be that Bulgarin has been granted a monopoly on political news? Can it really be that except for *The Northern Bee* not a single journal of ours dare announce that there has been an earthquake in Mexico and that the Chamber of Deputies is in recess until September?" Bulgarin made certain that this was true by his denunciations to the police, and other skillful journalists kept up a constant campaign of harassment, often with the connivance of the Government. Missed deadlines (due to the editors' amateurishness), battles with the censorship, and a relatively high price also took their toll. The newspaper attracted less than one hundred subscribers. After Del'vig's death, hastened, legend has it, by the temporary proscription of the newspaper and his official dismissal from the editorship in the autumn of 1830 after harsh questioning and threats by Benckendorff, Somov's and Pushkin's best efforts could not keep a commercial failure going.

The 1 January 1830 issue is open to one of the many notices that Pushkin left unsigned, to avoid censorship:

> Prince Viazemsky has translated and is soon to publish Benj. Constant's celebrated novel. *Adolphe* belongs to the number of *two* or *three* novels
>
> in which the epoch is reflected,
> and modern man
> rather correctly represented
> with his immoral soul,
> selfish and dry,
> to dreaming measurelessly given,
> with his embittered mind
> boiling in empty action.
>
> [*Onegin*, (tr. Nabokov) Seven, XXII,7-14]
>
> Benj. Constant was the first to bring out this character, which the genius of Lord Byron later popularized. We await the appearance of this book with impatience. It will be curious to see how the experienced and live pen of Prince Viazemsky has overcome the difficulty of [the work's] metaphysical language, always harmonious and urbane, often inspired. In this

respect the translation should be an original creation and an important event in the history of our literature.

Viazemsky's translation came out in the spring of 1830 with a dedication to Pushkin. Complete sets of all 108 numbers are extremely rare, especially when they include, as does the Diaghilev-Lifar copy, the numbers of vol. 3-4 issued after Del'vig's death.

60

ASP and P. A. Pletnev, *editors*, Northern flowers for 1832.

***Severnye tsvety na 1832 god.* St. Petersburg, 1831.**

Kilgour 1049

Del'vig edited only the first three issues of this "house almanac" of Pushkin and his closest friends. Orest Somov joined him as co-editor for the fourth through seventh volumes. Pushkin and Pletnev took Del'vig's place for this eighth and final volume after his death on 14 January 1831. It was published with all proceeds to go to Del'vig's family (sixty thousand rubles mysteriously disappeared from the writer's study the day after his death). "Poor Del'vig! Let us honor his memory with the *Northern Flowers*—but I would be sorry if this would be a loss for Somov [he did receive his usual salary for supervising the technical side]. He was sincerely attached to him—and the death of our friend is probably hardest of all on him: the feelings of the soul weaken and change; the necessities of life never doze off" (to Pletnev, 31 January 1831).

Pushkin contributed "Mozart and Salieri" and some of his finest new poems, among them "Anchar," "Echo," "Devils," and the "Anthological Epigrams." The most distinguished piece of prose (the Achilles' heel of all the almanacs at the time) was Odoevsky's "Opere del cavaliere Giambattista Piranesi."

61

ASP, *editor*, The Contemporary.

***Sovremennik*. v. 1. St. Petersburg, 1836.**

Kilgour 1124

On 7 June 1824, Pushkin wrote Viazemsky from Odessa: "Another misfortune: we are all accursed and scattered over the face of the earth—intercourse among us is difficult. . . . The first thing: all the journals must be sternly taken in hand—nothing would be easier if we were together and if we could publish on the morrow what we decided on at supper the day before." He and his friends had discussed founding a journal since 1819, and after 1824 the matter crops up in letters frequently. On 10 August 1825, after lamenting the deplorable state of literary discussion in the existing Russian periodicals, he concluded to Viazemsky: "Sometime we'll start a journal of our own! I want to so badly it hurts." Pushkin never abandoned the hope of founding a serious literary journal along the lines of *The Edinburgh Review*. Less than a year after the collapse of *The Literary Gazette*, he wrote to Benckendorff (27 May 1832) asking permission to publish a new journal, *Diary*, but he gave up on the idea after learning how closely the government would insist on supervising it (the provisional authorization was withdrawn in any event). He discussed it with friends again in 1835 and on 31 December 1835 wrote Benckendorff: "I make bold to trouble Your Excellency with a most humble request. I should like to publish during next year, 1836, four volumes of articles of a purely literary (e.g., stories, poems, etc.), historical, scholarly nature, as well as critical analyses of Russian and foreign literature; something on the order of the English quarterly reviews. By refusing to take part in all our journals, I have also been deprived of income. The publication of such a Review would again provide me with independence . . . ."

On 11 April 1836, the first issue of *The Contemporary, a Literary Journal Published by Aleksandr Pushkin* appeared in a printing of 2,400 copies and, unfortunately, at the high subscription price of 25 rubles (30 including postage). The dream of a forum not only for new literary works, but an organ of critical dialogue and principled criticism which would shape an educated reading public, was re-

СОВРЕМЕННИКЪ,

ЛИТТЕРАТУРНЫЙ ЖУРНАЛЪ,

ИЗДАВАЕМЫЙ

АЛЕКСАНДРОМЪ ПУШКИНЫМЪ.

ТОМЪ ПЕРВЫЙ.

САНКТПЕТЕРБУРГЪ.
1836.

alized. The first issue contained poems by Zhukovsky and Viazemsky, prose by Gogol ("The Carriage," "Morning of a Man of Business," the article "On the Development of Periodical Literature in 1834 and 1835," and reviews), and Pushkin's "Feast of Peter the First" (unsigned), "The Covetous Knight" (signed "P."), "From Chenier" (unsigned), and "A Journey to Erzerum," a beautiful prose account of his visit to the Caucasus in 1829. Pushkin also wrote most of the reviews.

If financial circumstances had played no small role in Pushkin's plan (although not a decisive one: Smirdin, after all, offered him fifteen thousand rubles not to start the venture), *The Contemporary* from the start proved a financial drain on the poet and could offer little hope to writers who wished to support themselves by their writing. It managed to attract only 700 subscribers the first year. Still, Pushkin carried on, despite wearying battles with the censorship and tedious editorial details. He managed to see four issues of the quarterly into print before his death. The third was particularly distinguished, with Gogol's brilliant story "The Nose" and fifteen of Tiutchev's finest lyrics, but by issue four only 900 copies were being printed. The journal, edited by Pletnev and supported by collaborators joined by bonds of long friendship and common literary views, limped along after Pushkin's death. N. A. Nekrasov and I. I. Panaev purchased it in 1846 and made it into Russia's most outstanding literary journal. The authorities suspended it in the summer of 1866.

62

Nikolai Vasil'evich Gogol (1809–52),
Arabesques.

Arabeski. **2 v.**
St. Petersburg, 1835.

Kilgour 342

Nikolai Gogol's "mystifications" (a politer expression than lies) about his relations with Pushkin present scholars with as many problems as everything else in the biography of Russia's greatest comic writer. Pushkin certainly had a high opinion of Gogol's comic genius. Gogol simply worshipped Pushkin and identified him with the ideal of the Russian poet. And at a time when even some of Pushkin's friends were calling him finished as a writer and none championed him publicly, Gogol launched a counterattack on his friend's behalf. The modestly titled "A Few Words About Pushkin" in the first volume of the peculiarly organized Arabesques, a melange of fiction and essays, is dated 1832, at the height of the journalistic campaign against Pushkin. In his lyrical apotheosis of Pushkin, Gogol — the first to do so — proclaimed him the incarnation of Russianness: "Russia's national poet". "Pushkin," he continued, "is an extraordinary phenomenon and perhaps the unique phenomenon of the Russian spirit: here is Russian man in all the fullness of his development, as he will perhaps appear two hundred years from now. [How characteristically Gogolian is the combination of the categorical and those provisional "perhaps's"!] Russian nature, the Russian soul, the Russian language and the Russian character have been reflected in him in just that purity and refined beauty with which a landscape is reflected in the convex surface of an optical glass." Dostoevsky would later drop the visual imagery so typical of Gogol, but would echo the hyperbolic sentiments.

· IX ·

HISTORY AND PROSE FICTION

One of Pushkin's earliest critical fragments (1822) concerned the deplorable state of Russian prose:

> Accuracy and brevity — these are the first virtues of prose. It demands ideas and ideas — without them brilliant expressions serve no purpose. Verses are another matter (although it wouldn't hurt our poets to have a much more significant sum of ideas than is usually found in them . . .). Question: whose prose is the best in our literature? Answer: *Karamzin's*. This, as yet, is no great praise.

While Russian writers of the eighteenth and early nineteenth centuries had produced interesting letters, essays, travel accounts, picaresque fictions, and satirical writings, it is true that the great age of Russian prose fiction still lay ahead and that the first memorable history, Karamzin's, had only just appeared.

Prose fiction, especially novels, stood at the very bottom of the neoclassical hierarchy of genres, if not altogether outside it. The sentimental strain of Russian literature that dominated the turn of the century had brought short fiction into vogue, and most of the best fictional prose during Pushkin's lifetime would continue to appear in short forms, which entered easily into almanacs or into cycles of stories. Karamzin, an important writer of short stories, reveals something of the regnant attitude toward the novel when he feels the need to justify reading Sir Walter Scott: "From ten to eleven thirty . . . the two girls, my wife, and I read Walter Scott — novels, but with innocent food for the imagination and heart" (letter to Ivan Dmitriev of 22 October 1825).

The European popularity of Scott's historical fiction helped overcome this aversion to fiction, and it spawned many Russian imitations, few of them so original or successful as Pushkin's *Captain's Daughter*. Scott's novels, the fascinating and disparate currents in European historiography, and the challenges to Karamzin's *History* that arose in the late 1820's all helped provoke Pushkin's own interest in history, which had begun in the early 1820's with his notes on Russian history of the eighteenth century (1822) and with *Boris Godunov*. His awareness of the events that had taken place during his own lifetime (such as the Napoleonic wars), his awareness of the marginality of his family and class, the failure of the Decembrist uprising (in which a number of his friends had taken part), the peasant uprisings of 1831, the Polish rebellion of that same year — all of these contributed to his growing interest in history, particularly the history of uprisings and cultural confrontations. His library testifies to his engagement with the most serious contemporary historians, Russian and European. Picking up

where Karamzin's *History* had left off, Pushkin's historical writings, fictional and non-fictional, addressed the major Russian conflicts from the early seventeenth century to his own period. Confrontations between nations, classes, and ethnic groups offered rich opportunities for his talents at cultural stylization.

W M T

63

ASP, The tales of the late Ivan Petrovich Belkin / published by A. P.

Povesti pokoinogo Ivana Petrovicha Belkina / izdannie A. P. St. Petersburg, 1831.

Kilgour 886

On 21 May 1824, Viazemsky wrote to Marc-Antoine Jullien de Paris (1775–1848), editor of the Paris *Revue encyclopédique*: "The moment we leave the cradle, we stammer verse! As for prose, which asks a better bringing-up, we come out rather badly, and apart from the *History of Russia* by Mr. Karamzin, we can boldly assert that we do not have a single sizable work in prose, and even this work is a precocious production of ours, which has been better appreciated in Europe than in Russia." (Kilgour 1347; published in *Russian Literary Archives*, N.Y., 1956). A year later Bestuzhev described Russian prose as a "steppe, occasionally enlivened by the swift passage of journalistic Bedouins or ponderously moving caravans of translations," while Nadezhdin saw only a "confusion of all the European idioms that have overgrown in successive layers the wild mass of the undeveloped Russian word."

As the "years to sober prose incline[d]" (*Eugene Onegin*, Six, XLIII,5), Pushkin very consciously set out to do something about a situation in which fiction of a sort flourished only in numbers. From 1830 until his death, he experimented with the widest variety of prose genres — the short story, historical novel, biography, history, essay, and travel notes. He wrote the five *Tales of Belkin*, "the first stories of permanent artistic value in the Russian language" (Nabokov), in those "magic months" of September to November 1830, the most fertile autumn in his creative life, at his father's estate of Boldino. Their pseudonymous publication in October 1831 by the publisher and bookseller Adol'f Pliushar, with Pushkin masking as the publisher only of the tales of his "late friend," reveals the precarious status of prose fiction at the time. Pushkin wished to avoid controversy (" . . . we shall publish [them] *Anonyme*. It will be impossible under my name, for Bulgarin would tear me to pieces [at the thought of the poet deigning to 'sully' his hands with prose]" — letter to Pletnev, 9 December 1830) and also to escape the censorship of Benckendorff and Nicholas.

64

ASP, History of the Pugachev rebellion.

Istoriia Pugachevskogo bunta. 2 v. St. Petersburg, 1834.

Kilgour 887

During the last years of his life, Pushkin, building on the foundations laid in *Boris Godunov*, devoted a large amount of his time to serious historical investigations. In 1831 Nicholas granted him access to the state archives to work on a history of Peter the Great and his successors. That project was never completed, and his interest shifted to the time of Catherine II. In 1833 he used the notes he had taken over several months of digging in the archives, corresponding with eyewitnesses, and visiting the actual scenes of major events to compose the tersely written two-volume *History of the Pugachev Rebellion.* The events of the uprising led by the Cossack Emelian Pugachev (ca. 1742–75) are set out in strict chronological order in part one and given copious documentation in part two. Pushkin's name appears only as the signature to the preface, dated "2 November 1833, the village of Boldino." Nicholas loaned him twenty thousand rubles to publish the work, with the provison that it be called the history of the Pugachev "rebellion." Pushkin had

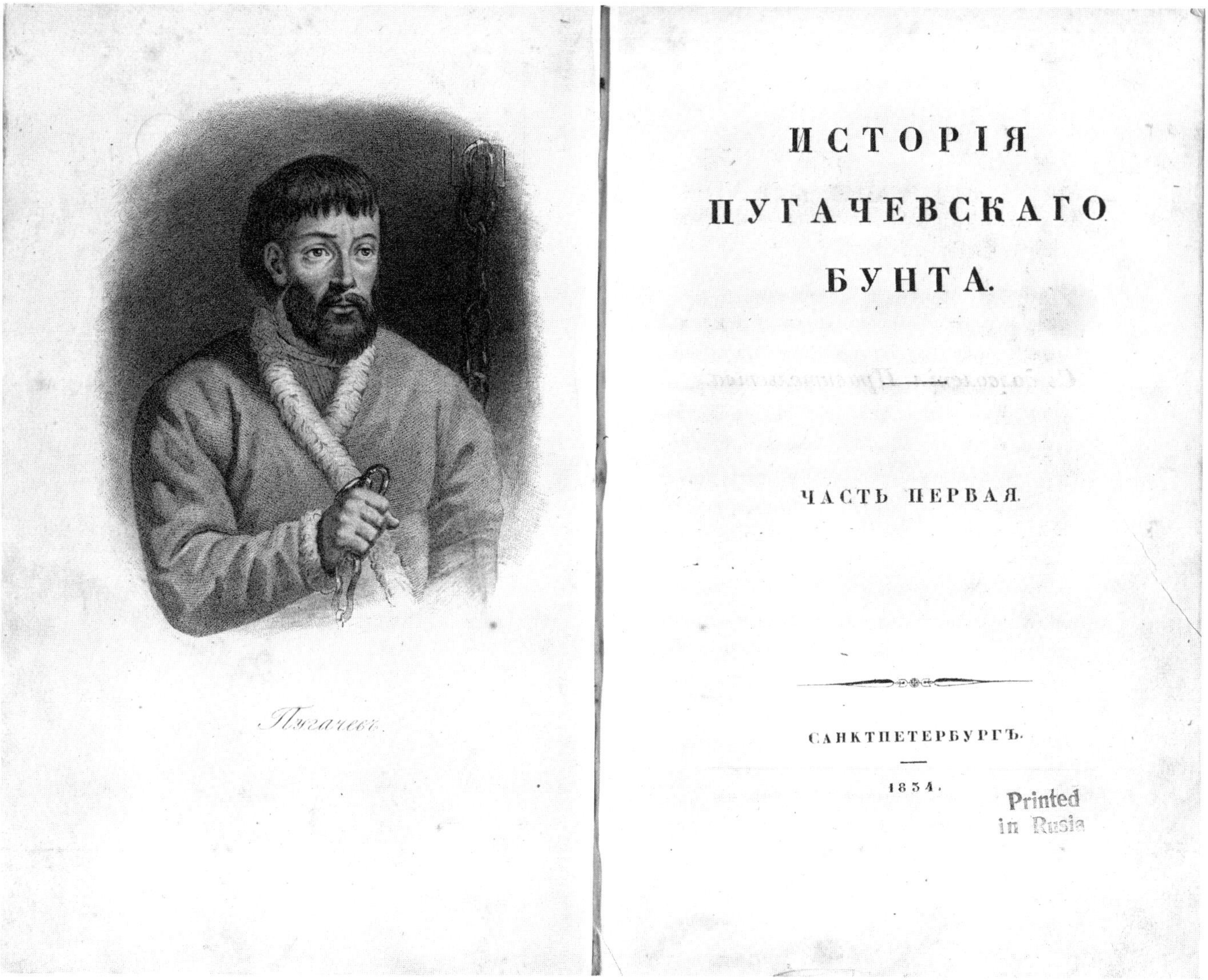

intended to entitle it simply "The History of Pugachev" or "The History of the Pugachevshchina." The writer's correspondence reveals how meticulously he supervised every aspect of the actual printing at the press of the Second Section of His Majesty's Own Chancery, right down to size and quality of paper. Most of the 3,000 copies were still unsold at the time of Pushkin's death.

The first part is open to an engraved portrait of Pugachev facing the title page. Part two is open to one of the plates included in the edition, a map of the provinces in which the rebellion and subsequent campaign to suppress it took place.

65

ASP, The captain's daughter (autograph manuscript)

Kapitanskaia dochka.

Kilgour 1338

Pushkin originally set out to depict the Pugachev uprising through the eyes of a fictional eyewitness, the young officer Grinev, caught up in the national crisis that threatened to topple Catherine from the throne. He put it aside in 1833 to concentrate on the *History*. The experience and complex understanding he gained from writing that historical account may well be reflected in the multiple perspective deployed in the compressed fictional counterpart: Grinev as actual participant, shuffling back and forth between rebel and government camps as he attempts to save himself and his fiancée; Grinev as an old man reflecting on events from an Enlightenment point of view; and the "editor's" point of view in the 1830's, which had experienced the rise of Romantic historiography. The novel appeared for the first time in the fourth issue of *The Contemporary* (1836).

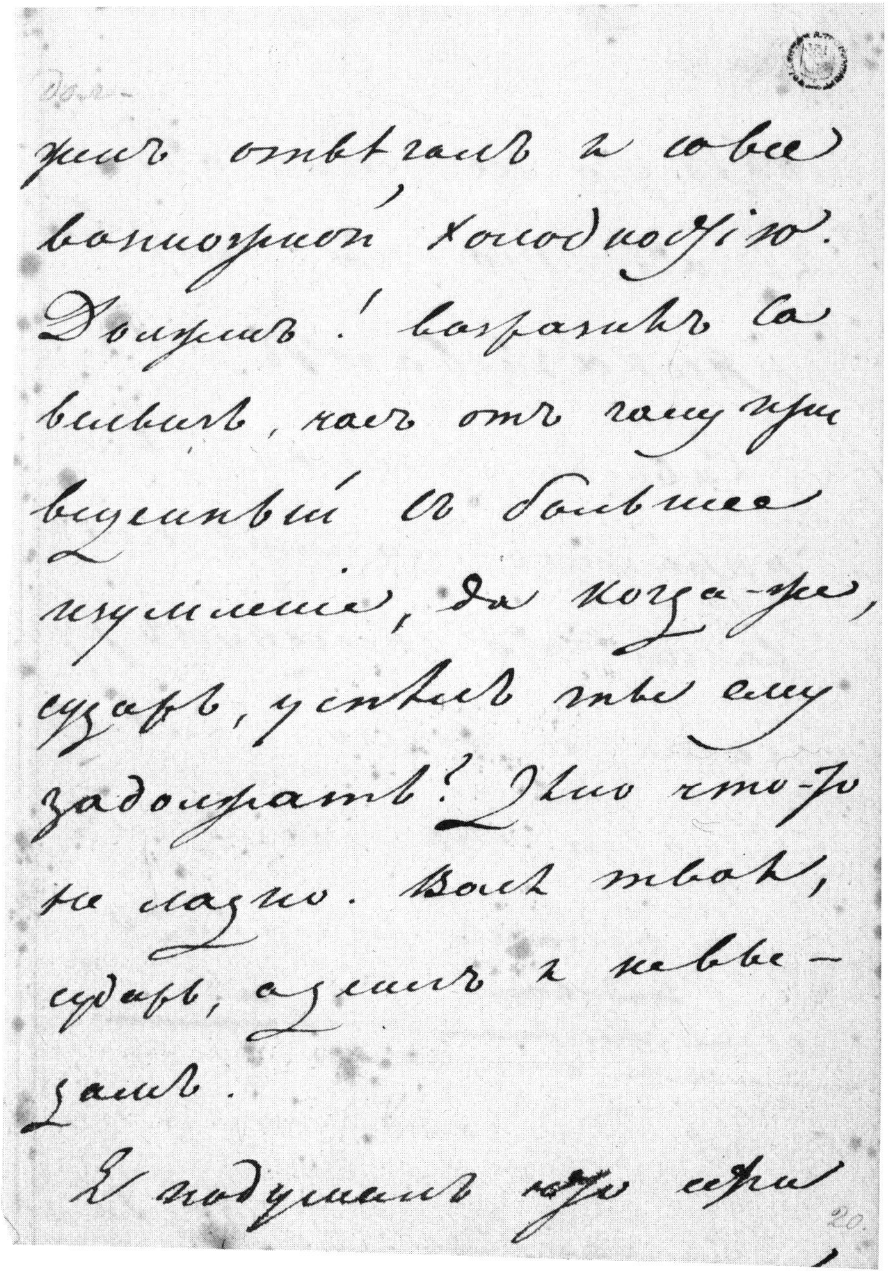

The Kilgour fragment contains two discontinuous passages that appear toward the end of Chapter One. There are no drafts of these texts in Soviet archives. The text does not differ from the published version.

66

V. A. Zhukovsky, and ASP, On the capture of Warsaw : three poems by V. Zhukovsky and A. Pushkin.

Na vziatie Varshavy : tri stikhotvoreniia V. Zhukovskogo i A. Pushkina.
St. Petersburg, 1831.

Kilgour 885

Ivan Kireevsky had announced in 1832 that the great age of verse had passed and that the spirit of the times was characterized by a "prosaic quality." Pushkin, however, by no means abandoned poetry in the 1830's, and on occasion his historical obsession found expression in verse. On 17 November 1830, insurrection against Russian occupation erupted in Warsaw. The Polish parliament proclaimed the end of Romanov rule and the vacancy of the Polish throne. The press in France and England called for intervention on Poland's behalf, but some nine months later the revolt was suppressed with great cruelty. The fiercely patriotic Pushkin closely followed the Russian campaign, which brought out his worst imperialist sentiments. He responded to West European denunciations of Russian actions with a saber-rattling survey of the old "quarrel of the Slavs amongst themselves": "To the Slanderers of Russia," dated 16 August 1831:

> What are you clamoring about, bards of the people?
> Why do you threaten Russia with anathema? . . .
> You menace us with words—just try them out in action! . . .
> Then send us, O bards,
> Your enraged sons: there is room for them in Russia's fields,
> In the midst of graves not unknown to them.

On 5 September Zhukovsky responded to the news of the capture of Warsaw with "An Old Song to a New Tune" and Pushkin with the odic "Anniversary of Borodino." The Government rushed into print a pamphlet containing all three poems (censor's permission 7 September 1831). Pushkin's close friends found the poems' nationalist fervor and mockery of the "arrogant Pole" embarrassing and distasteful ("in regard to Poland he is a barbarian," Aleksandr Turgenev to his brother Nikolai, 2 September 1832).

67

ASP, Tales.

Povesti.
St. Petersburg, 1834.

Kilgour 888

"I beg to disturb Your Excellency with a most humble request for permission for me to reprint, in one volume, my compositions in prose which have been published up to now" (letter to Aleksandr Mordvinov, a subordinate of Benckendorff, 26 May 1834). The *Tales* (censor's permission 19 July 1834) contained the second edition of the Belkin Tales, "Two Chapters from a Historical Novel [*The Blackamoor of Peter the Great*]", and Pushkin's prose masterpiece "The Queen of Spades," Written in 1833 and first published in *The Library for Reading*, Vol. II, Book three (March, 1834).

68

F. V. Bulgarin, Ivan Vyzhigin : a didactic-satirical novel.

Ivan Vyzhigin : nravstvenno-satiricheskii roman.
4 pts. in 2 v.
St. Petersburg, 1829.

Kilgour 193

Bulgarin's very mediocre picaresque *Ivan Vyzhigin* was the first nineteenth-century Russian novel to enjoy real commercial success with the educated, Westernized public. 7,000 copies were sold in two days and the first edition sold out in a week. Pushkin's response was to compose the contents for a novel entitled "The Real Vyzhigin: a Historico-Didactic-Satiric Novel of the Nineteenth Century." The lampoon, published in *The Telescope* under the pseudonym "Feofilakt Kosichkin," outlines the life of the "real Vyzhigin," i.e., Bulgarin himself, who is identified with the central rogue of his own creation.

Harvard also owns a two-volume English translation, *Ivan Vejeeghen, or Life in Russia*, published in London in 1831, the 1832 Philadelphia reprinting, and, in the Kilgour collection, the second, revised Russian edition (1829).

No.68

69

Mikhail Nikolaevich Zagoskin (1789–1852), Iurii Miloslavsky, or, The Russians in 1612.

Iurii Miloslavsky, ili, russkie v 1612 godu. **3 v.**
Moscow, 1829.

Kilgour 1270

On 11 January 1830 Pushkin wrote to Zagoskin, Director of the Office of Moscow Theaters, to thank him for sending his historical novel *Iurii Miloslavsky.* "I congratulate you on your complete and deserved success, and the public on one of the best novels of the present epoch. Everybody is reading it. Zhukovsky spent a whole night at it. The ladies are in rapture over it. There will be an article about it by Pogorelsky [the pseudonym of Aleksei Perovsky] in *The Literary Gazette.*" Pushkin himself, not Pogorelsky, wrote the review. It appeared 21 January, in the fifth issue of the newspaper. "Today by the word *novel* we understand an historical epoch described in a fictitious narrative. Walter Scott attracted a whole host of imitators. But how far removed are they from the Scottish wizard! . . . None of these reproaches apply to *Iurii Miloslavsky.* Mr. Zagoskin accurately transports us to the year 1612. . . . How vivid, how absorbing are the scenes of Old Russian life! How much truth and good-natured fun in the description of the characters! . . . . The novel's action effortlessly falls into the frame of the historical events. The author does not hurry with his story, he lingers over details, has a look at peripheral matters, but never wearies the reader's attention. The dialogue (everywhere lively and dramatic when it is in the idiom of the people) reveals a master of his craft. . . . Minor errors cannot harm the brilliant, fully deserved success of *Iurii Miloslavsky.*" The success of the novel (four editions in three years) ushered in a whole series of Russian historical novels in the 1830's.

ЮРІЙ МИЛОСЛАВСКІЙ

или

РУСКІЕ ВЪ 1612 ГОДУ.

Часть I.

МОСКВА.

70

N. V. Gogol, Evenings on a farm near Dikanka.

Vechera na khutore bliz Dikan'ki.
St. Petersburg, 1831.

Kilgour 340

These "Tales published by the beekeeper Rudyi Pan'ko" (Gogol's name appears nowhere in the book) delighted a Russian public eager for something fresh and new. In a letter to the editor of the Literary Supplement to *The Russian Invalid* (published there in issue No. 79, 1831, as a kind of illustration to a review of the *Evenings*), Pushkin wrote: "I have just read *Evenings Near Dikanka.* They astonished me. Here is genuine gaiety, sincere, unforced, without affectation, without primness. And in places what poetry! What sensitivity! All this is so unusual in our current literature that I haven't yet come to my senses. I have been told that when the publisher [Gogol] entered the printing-house where the *Evenings* were being set, the compositors began to giggle and snort, covering their mouths with their hands. The foreman explained their mirth, confessing to him that the com-

ЮРІЙ МИЛОСЛАВСКІЙ

ИЛИ

РУСКІЕ ВЪ 1612 ГОДУ.

Часть II.

МОСКВА.

ЮРІЙ МИЛОСЛАВСКІЙ

ИЛИ

РУСКІЕ ВЪ 1612 ГОДУ.

Часть III.

МОСКВА.

positors were dying of laughter as they set his book in print. Molière and Fielding, no doubt, would have been glad to amuse their compositors. . . . For God's sake take [the author's] side if journalists, in their customary manner, attack the *indecency* of his expressions, the *bad form*, etc. It is high time that we mocked our literature's *précieuses ridicules*, who are forever talking of their fair readers, whom they never had, of high society, to which they are not invited, and all this in the style of Professor Trediakovsky's valet." Pushkin repeated his warm praise for "a Russian book that made us laugh (and we haven't laughed since Fonvizin)" in a review of the second edition of the *Evenings*, in the first issue of *The Contemporary*, adding that their author "had continually developed and improved" since then and "was still advancing."

·X·

CANONIZATION

"Pushkin" as we know him today is the product of over a century and a half of reading, hearsay, interpretation, scholarship, veneration, myth-making, irreverent joking, and even rejection. "Pushkin" remains a contested ground—between those who seek a single meaning to his work and those who deny this possibility, between representatives of various ideologies, between Soviets and émigrés, and between representatives of the state, church, party, and of the intelligentsia. Canonization—which was foreshadowed by Gogol's encomium and by the public outpouring of grief at the poet's death, which began with the gathering of collected editions and biographical materials, which was asserted and reasserted by a series of festivals and jubilees (1880, 1887, 1899, 1921, 1924, 1937, 1949, 1987), and which is supported by the Institute of Russian Literature (Pushkin House) of the Soviet Academy of Sciences—has not established a single image of Pushkin or reading of his oeuvre. It has, instead, determined that a certain body of texts, written by Pushkin, shall serve as an enduring standard of literary excellence and as the focal point of continuing debates about the most pressing cultural problems. When official or unofficial pieties have threatened to dull the provocative vitality of these texts, some of the most brilliant Russian writers and critics—Vladimir Solov'ev, Valerii Briusov, Roman Jakobson, Viktor Shklovsky, and Andrei Siniavsky (Tertz) among them—have intervened to liberate their power.

WMT

71

The Contemporary, v. 5.

Sovremennik. v. 5.
St. Petersburg, 1837.

Kilgour 1124

After Pushkin's death on 29 January 1837, Nicholas I, who had treated him so demeaningly in life, granted his widow a substantial pension, provided allowances for his children, paid off his father's debts, and "graciously" allowed the continuation of *The Contemporary* in order further to aid the family. Early in June, subscribers received issue number five (the first for 1837), edited by Viazemsky, Zhukovsky, Odoevsky, Pletnev, and Andrei Kraevsky. Works by Pushkin's close friends graced the volume (Zhukovsky's famous poem "The Little Flower" and Baratynsky's masterpiece "Autumn"), but it was in all but name dedicated to the poet's memory. It was dominated by his verse (his three last poems, for example; the autograph of one of them, "A Prayer" ["Desert fathers and virtuous women . . ."] was reproduced on a foldout lithograph) and prose ("Scenes from Knightly Times" and the fine essay "On Milton and on Chateaubriand's translation of Paradise Lost," among others). Viazemsky's "In Memoriam" (ending with "Our beloved poet has fallen silent forever, Grief has befallen us, for Pushkin is no longer") and Zhukovsky's unsigned "Pushkin's Final Minutes," a moving account of the poet's death and funeral (excerpted from his 15 February letter to Pushkin's father) made the focus of the issue clear. As Tiutchev wrote to Viazemsky on 11 June: "This is truly a *book from beyond the grave*." Further issues of the journal in 1837 contained important first publications of Pushkin's verse and prose, fortunately without the

No.71:
From H. F. von Storch, *Gemaehlde von St. Petersburg* (Riga, 1794)

extraordinary number of misprints which marred No. V (and which would have so irritated the fastidious craftsman Pushkin).

The volume is dominated by *The Bronze Horseman*, one of Pushkin's supreme masterpieces and the progenitor of a potent literary myth. Only a fragment (most of the "Introduction") of this "Petersburg tale" had appeared in print during Pushkin's lifetime because of the objections of Nicholas (in *The Library for Reading*, XII, 1834). Zhukovsky managed to satisfy Nicholas' demands by rewriting several offending lines, and included the whole work in the issue. His emendations and excisions from this and other of Pushkin's posthumously published works were not corrected until many decades later.

72

ASP, Works.

Sochineniia. 11 v.
St. Petersburg, 1838–41.

Kilgour 890 (bound in 6 v.)

On Sunday, 7 February 1837, Zhukovsky and Major-General Leontii Dubel't (1792–1862), an assistant of Benckendorff in the Third Section, unsealed Pushkin's study and removed all of his papers in two trunks to Zhukovsky's apartment, where they were again placed under the seals of both men. For almost three weeks (8–25 February), Zhukovsky was forced to witness Dubel't's humiliating "posthumous police search" (as the Pushkinist M. A. Tsiavlovsky put it) of Pushkin's private papers. Zhukovsky refused categorically to read any of the letters and busied himself with sorting and ordering the poet's manuscripts for a collected edition that was to be printed at government expense to aid the family. It was announced at the end of issue V of *The Contemporary*. Eight volumes of Pushkin's previously published works were quickly readied and approved (censor's permission 3 April 1837), but they came out only in 1838, with no indication of Zhukovsky's planning of the volumes. Three final volumes, primarily composed of posthumously published works, appeared only in 1841 (censor's permission 29 April 1840). They were published by subscription by "Il'ia Glazunov, Matvei Zaikin, and Co." This is the "complete collected works in the latest edition" that Varvara buys for the poor "eternal student" Pokrovsky in Dostoevsky's novel *Poor Folk* (1847): "Alas! The price for all eleven volumes, including the cost of binding, was at least sixty rubles."

Volume I is open to the title page and Nikolai Utkin's facing engraved portrait of the writer. Volume XI is open to the subscription list, which contains some of the most famous titled names in Russia, as well as several libraries, high schools, and military units, but, curiously, none of Pushkin's closest friends.

No. 72

73

ASP, Works (ed. Annenkov)

Sochineniia. 7 v.
St. Petersburg, 1855–57.

Pavel Vasil'evich Annenkov (1813–87), literary critic and memoirist, prepared the first true scholarly edition of "The Works of Pushkin, with the addition of materials for his biography, of his portrait, of prints of his handwriting and of his drawings, etc." in the 1850's and brought out six volumes himself in 1855. A supplementary seventh volume appeared in 1857. His *Materials for a Biography of A. S. Pushkin* takes up the entire first volume. It remains a significant source for Pushkin studies and a landmark for the perception of Pushkin as a writer with a "creative biography," and it has recently been reprinted in the Soviet Union. Annenkov received an honorary degree from Moscow University during the 1880 Pushkin celebrations, in which he played an active role. His edition marks a major transition not only to the scholarly study of Pushkin, but to canonization.

74

Celebration of the inauguration of the monument to A. S. Pushkin in Moscow, 6 June 1880.

Torzhestvo otkrytiia pamiatnika A. S. Pushkinu v Moskve 6 iiunia 1880g.
Moscow, 1880.

Kilgour 895

The unveiling of A. M. Opekushin's (1838–1923) Pushkin monument, paid for by public subscription, in a central Moscow square, marks his final elevation to cult status. Three days in June were set aside for the festivities. The Society of the Amateurs of Russian Literature organized banquets, a book exhibit, concerts of music set to his texts (including a cantata to "Exegi Monumentum"), two "Pushkin Evenings," and two gala public meetings. At the first of these, on 7 June, Turgenev made a well-received speech, but his success was entirely overshadowed by the acclaim that greeted Dostoevsky's politico-patriotic speech the next day, at a meeting where Maikov and Polonsky also read poems written for the occasion. No one noted the errors of fact, which make one wonder when Dostoevsky had last read *Eugene Onegin*. His "inspired" apotheosis of Tatiana as a "positive Russian woman" and Pushkin as a "prophecy and revelation" "evoked extraordinary public enthusiasm," as the anonymous author of the booklet describing the festivities noted.

The text of Dostoevsky's speech was printed in full in this booklet (only excerpts from Turgenev's are given) and this may be its first publication (censorship date 12 June 1880; this copy was posted on 17 July 1880), although priority is usually given to the 18 June 1880 issue of *The Moscow Gazette* (No. 162). While the account remarks that "it is impossible to convey Dostoevsky's speech; anything more brilliant cannot be imagined," it is worth giving its central thesis:

> I assert emphatically that never has there been a poet with such a universal responsiveness as Pushkin. But it is not only a matter of susceptibility but also of amazing depth—that reincarnation in his spirit of the spirit of foreign nations, an almost complete, and therefore miraculous, reincarnation. This phenomenon has been revealed in no other poet in the world. This we find in Pushkin alone, and in this sense he is a unique and unheard-of phenomenon, and to my mind, a prophetic one . . . since it is exactly in this that his national, Russian strength revealed itself most—the national character of his poetry, the national spirit in its future development and in our future, which is concealed in that which is already present—and this has been prophetically revealed by Pushkin. For what else is the strength of the Russian national spirit than the aspiration, in its ultimate goal, for universality and an all-embracing humanitarianism?

Dostoevsky read Pushkin's "Prophet" at the final Pushkin evening and placed a wreath on a bust of Pushkin set on a pedestal that dominated the hall.

Памятникъ А. С. Пушкину въ Москвѣ.

No. 74:
Opekushin's monument to Pushkin

75

ASP, The Unpublished Pushkin; The Gabrieliad.

***Neizdannyi Pushkin.* Petersburg, 1922. *Gavriliada.* Petersburg, 1922.**

Kilgour 903 and 902

With the uncovering of more and more of Pushkin's manuscripts and letters, a process that continues to our day, each edition of his works has become more complete and authoritative textually. When Pushkin House acquired the collection of A. F. Otto (1844–1925; he changed his last name to Onegin out of devotion to Pushkin) in 1909, one of the last great troves of Pushkin papers in private hands could be examined by scholars at leisure. Thirteen years later, M. L. Gofman, N. K. Kozmin, and B. L. Modzalevsky issued the results of their meticulous work in *The Unpublished Pushkin*, printed on fine-quality paper (a rarity at the time) and with foldout reproductions of various autographs.

The Kilgour collection possesses several émigré editions containing works by Pushkin and other poets that the censorship barred from publication inside Russia (nos. 891, 892, 894). The liberalized censorship code introduced after 1905 allowed most of these works to appear in Russia, but one work remained beyond the pale until 1917: the "Gabriel poem," *Gavriliada*, Pushkin's burlesque of the story of the Annunciation "pleasantly depicting in the irreligious and elegantly lewd style of his French models [Voltaire and Parny] an intrigue between the Archangel and the old carpenter's young wife" (Nabokov). Pushkin wrote it in the spring of 1821, knowing full well that it could not be published. He sent it to Viazemsky on 1 September 1822, after which manuscript copies began circulating widely. The poet was in serious trouble when one copy of the impious poem came to the attention of the police in June 1828. He at first denied authorship, but on 2 October he apparently wrote Nicholas a frank, repentant letter (it has not survived) and was pardoned for his youthful indiscretion. At least on 31 December 1828, the Emperor declared: "I am fully acquainted with this case and it is absolutely closed." The poem became a clandestine classic for generations of readers, who knew it from émigré editions. The first legal Russian edition, with notes and an introduction by the Symbolist poet Valerii Briusov, came out in Moscow only in 1918. Pushkin himself destroyed the only autograph of the poem, and Boris Tomashevsky had to rely on comparison of a variety of copies when he prepared his critical edition. It appeared in 1922, with extensive commentary, notes on variants, and a very serious preface, in which Tomashevsky declared that his purpose in publishing the work was purely "scientific," not "titillating." The critic's textological labors are still considered definitive.

76

ASP, Secular power (autograph manuscript).

Mirskaia vlast'. (1836)

Kilgour 1339

Scholars long knew "Secular Power," one of Pushkin's last poems, only from copies made from an "original copy" of the autograph ordered by Zhukovsky when he prepared the posthumous edition of the poet's collected works. The censorship did not allow printing of the poem there. Its first six lines appeared only in 1855, when Annenkov cited them in his *Materials for a Biography of A. S. Pushkin.* Alexander Herzen published a complete text for the first time in London in his *Polar Star for 1856* (Book Two). Annenkov included a partial text (ll. 1–11, 14–18, without title) in the 1857 supplemental volume (VII) to his edition of Pushkin's works. The censor finally permitted full publication of the text in 1870, in volume one of the Works, ed. G. N. Gennadi. All subsequent editions, including that of the Soviet Academy of Sciences, had to rely on the copies published by Annenkov and Herzen.

The discovery of the autograph of the poem in the 1950's revealed how carelessly the various copies had been made. N. V. Izmailov first described the autograph in 1954 (*Izvestiia Akademii nauk SSSR, otdelenie literatury i iazyka*, t. 13, vyp. 6), when a photocopy was sent to Leningrad's Pushkin House. All editions now base their publication of "Secular Power" on this text, the only known autograph, acquired by Mr. Kilgour from Serge Lifar.

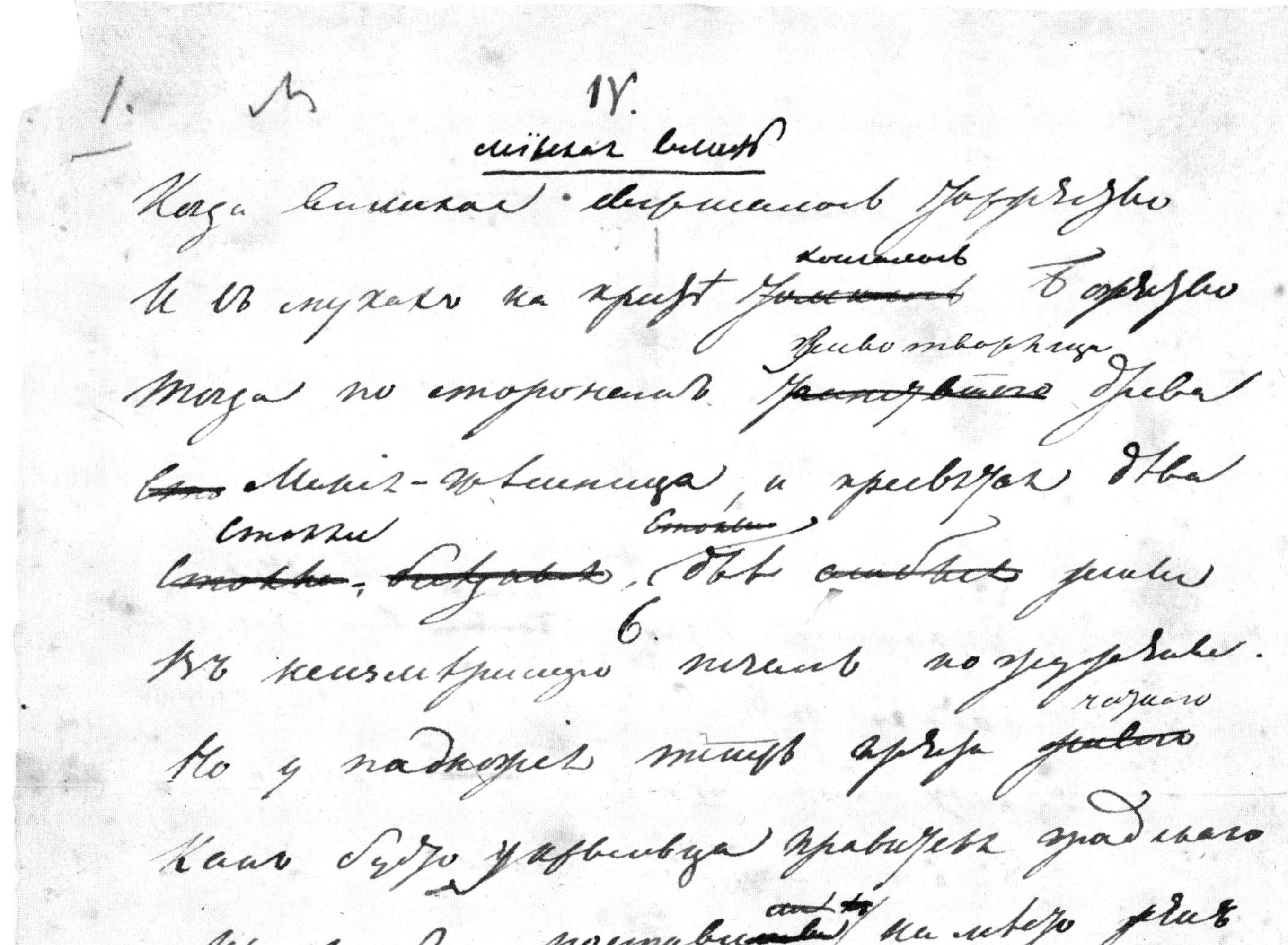

IV.

Мірская власть

Когда великое свершалось торжество
И въ мукахъ на крестѣ кончалось Божество
Тогда по сторонамъ животворяща древа
Марія-грѣшница и пресвятая дѣва
Стояли, блѣдныя, двѣ слабыя жены
Въ неизмѣримую печаль погружены.
Но у подножія теперь креста честнаго
Какъ будто у крыльца правителя градскаго
Мы зримъ — поставлено на мѣсто женъ святыхъ
Въ ружьѣ и киверѣ двухъ грозныхъ часовыхъ.
Къ чему, скажите мнѣ, хранительная стража? —
Или распятіе казенная поклажа
И вы боитеся воровъ или мышей? —
Иль мните важности придать Царю царей?

No. 76

77

ASP, The song of Oleg the Seer; The tale of Tsar Saltan; and The tale of the golden cockerel.

Pesn' o veshchem Olege. St. Petersburg, [1901?].
Skazka o tsare Saltane . . . St. Petersburg, [1906?].
Skazka o zolotom petushke. St. Petersburg, [1910?].

Kilgour 897, 898, and 901

Pushkin's works have inspired generations of Russian artists, many of whom have illustrated special editions of his novels, narrative poems, and tales. In 1899 a Special Commission of the Imperial Academy of Sciences ordered several such books from leading artists to mark the one hundredth anniversary of Pushkin's birth. Viktor Vasnetzov (1848–1926), famous for his canvases on ancient Russian historical and legendary subjects, chose *The Song of Oleg the Seer* (1822), a heroic ballad based on an incident in the *Primary Chronicle* about Oleg, Prince of Kiev, fatally bitten by a snake which had lurked in the skull of his dead charger, whom, soothsayers had warned, would kill him.

Several years later, Ivan Bilibin (1876–1942) was drawn to Pushkin's assimilation of national and European traditions in the "fairy tales" (*skazki*) to express his own love for the art of seventeenth-century Russia, which he described as "that enchanted fairy-tale period in the history of folk art." In *The Tale of Tsar Saltan* (written in 1831), illustrated between 1904–05, Bilibin failed to attain full stylistic unity (the cask drifting on the sea in one illustration is far too reminiscent of Hokusai). He achieved it in the masterful illustrations (1906–07) for *The Tale of the Golden Cockerel* (written in 1834), in which he successfully fused various influences, ranging from the Russian popular print (*lubok*) to the Art Nouveau. Both folio-size paperbacks, with the type set in three columns, and drawings and text perfectly integrated, are from the collection of Philip Hofer.

SELECTIVE INDEX

Note: The number refers to the commentary on the exhibit (in arabic) or the case (in roman); 36(1), etc. refers to the commentary on Chapters 1, etc. of *Eugene Onegin*. The number is italicized if the reference is to the item exhibited or the subject of the case.

The index includes the authors or editors of exhibits, the Russian titles of periodicals and almanacs exhibited, the names of Pushkin's correspondents and (under ASP) the titles in Russian and English of works exhibited or mentioned in the text. I have also indexed selected illustrators, publishers, and significant contemporaries.

H A

ПОЛЯРНАЯ ЗВѢЗДА
1825
С. Петербургъ.